The
Drawing book
for
KIDS

30 daily things to drew: step by step for beginners

All rights reserved ©

How to use this book

All you need is a pencil, eraser, and peace of paper!

Follow each drawing diagram step by step

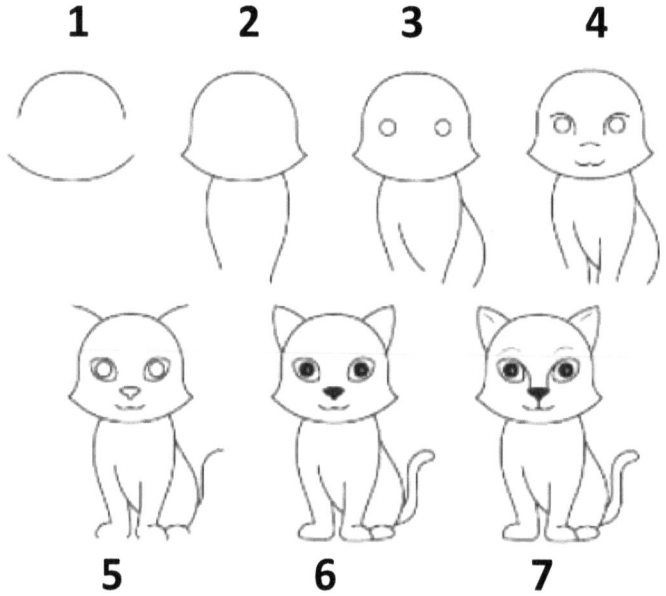

Tips:

Draw lightly at first, because you might need to erase some lines as you work.

Add details according to the diagrams, but don't worry about being perfect !! Artists frequently make mistakes, they just find ways to make their mistakes look interesting.

Don't worry if your drawing don't turn out the way you want them to, just keep practicing ! Sometimes drawing the same thing just a few times will help.

Once you've finished your drawing in pencil you can trace it with a black fine liner pen and color or paint to your linking

Turn the page for some cool composition ideas !!

How to Draw a Lion

Use these instructions to help you draw a simple lion.

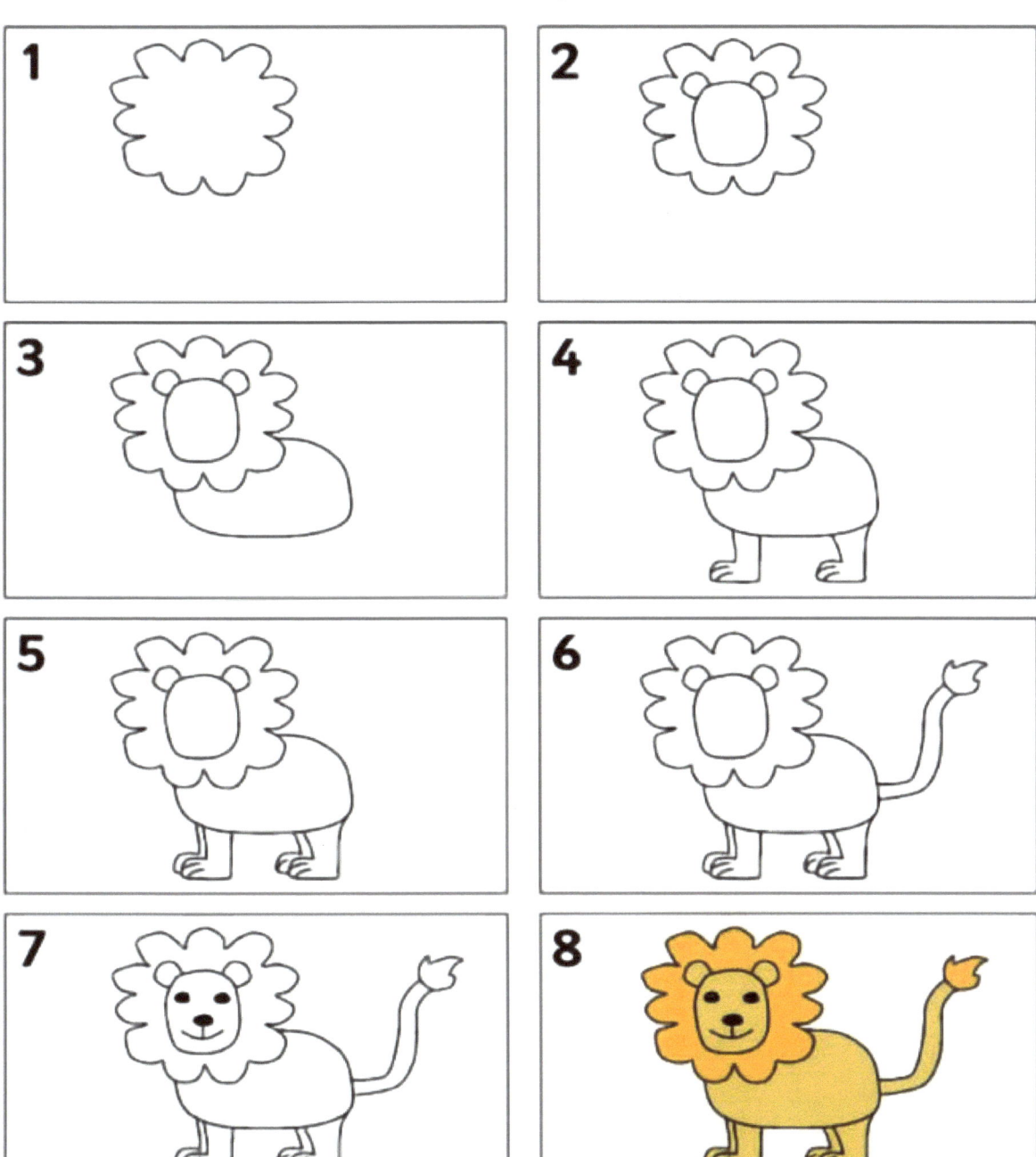

How to Draw a Frog

Use these instructions to help you draw a simple cartoon frog:

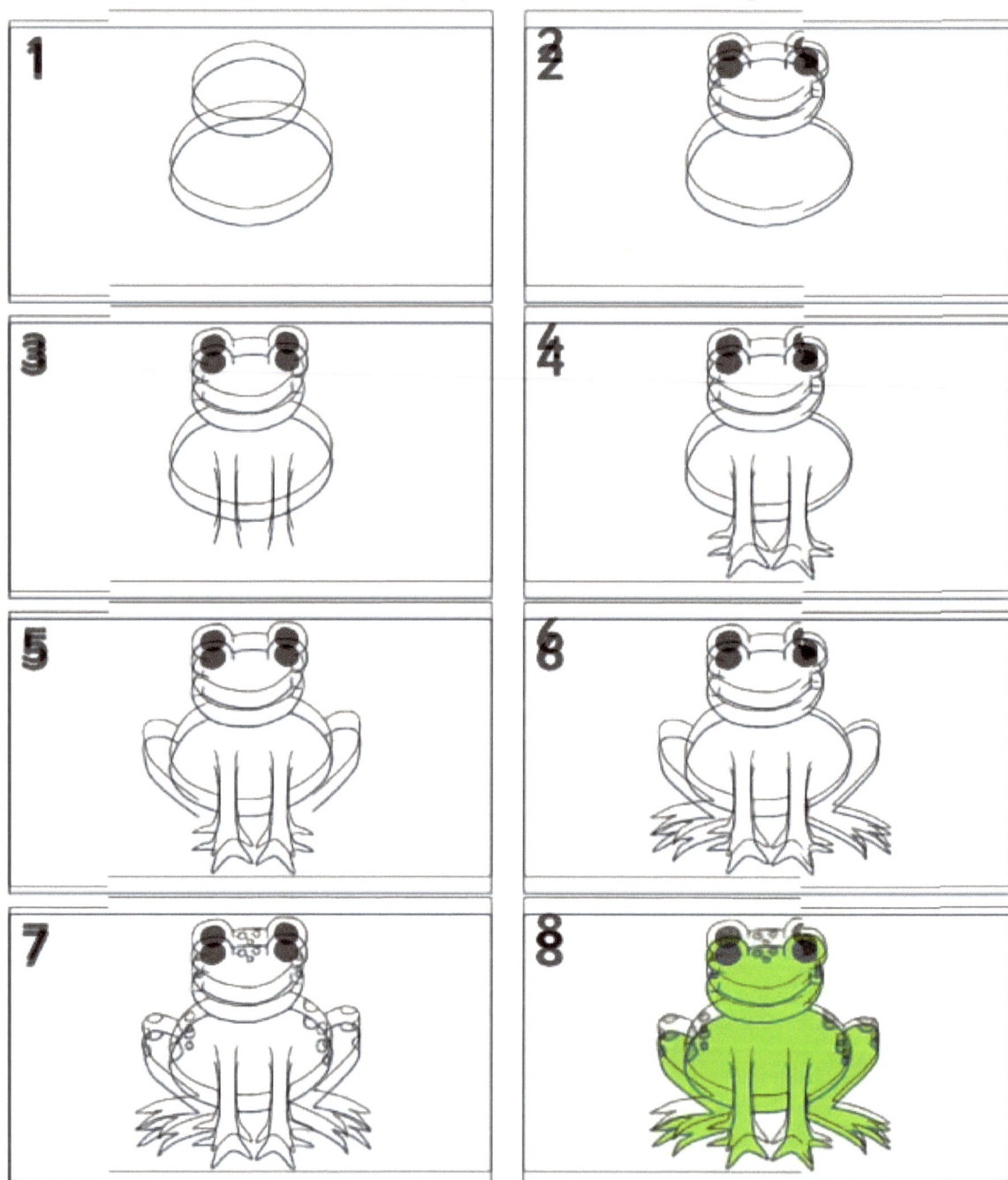

How to Draw a Fish

Use these instructions to help you draw a simple cartoon fish:

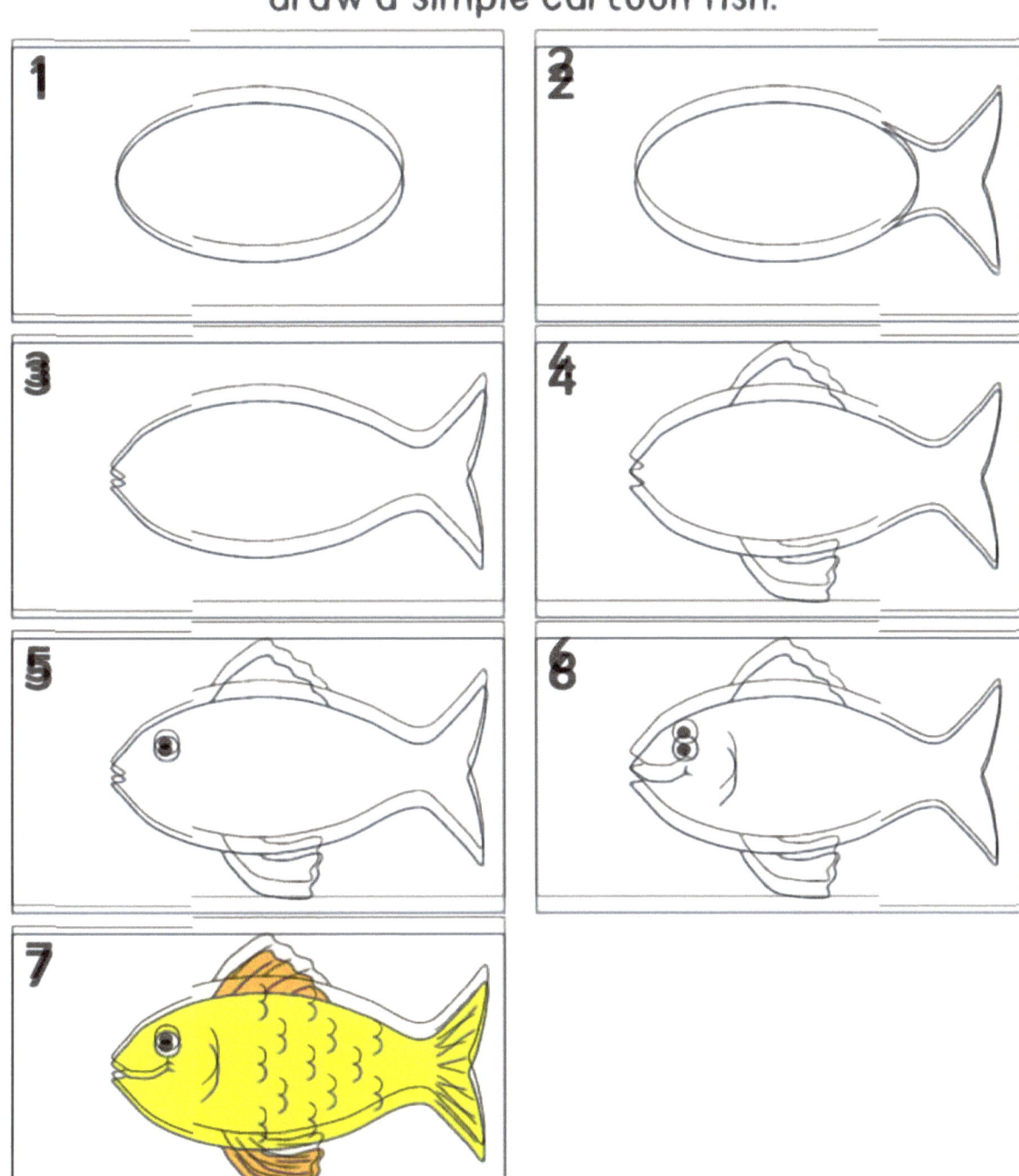

How to Draw a Cat

Use these instructions to help you draw a simple cartoon cat.

1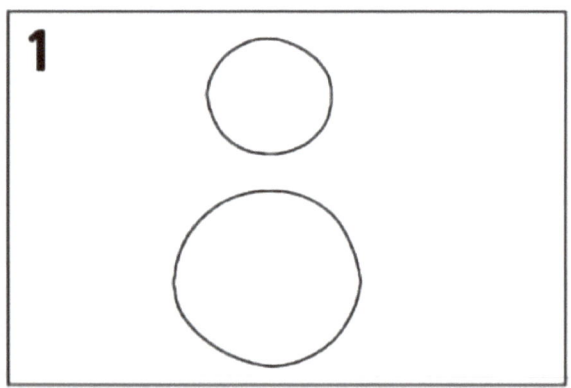

2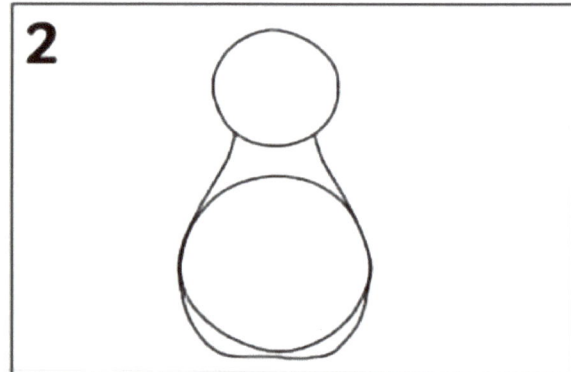

3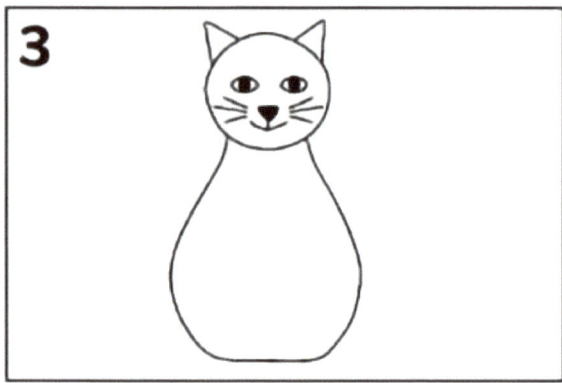

4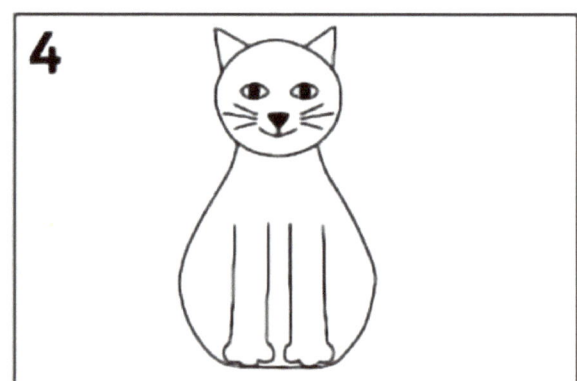

5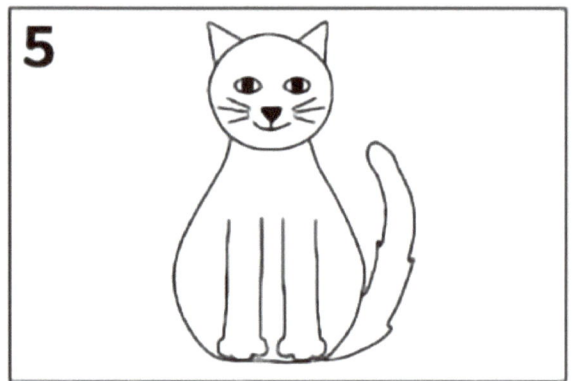

6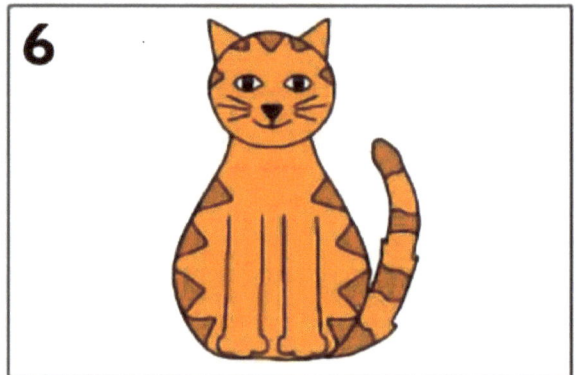

How to Draw a Dog

Use these instructions to help you draw a simple cartoon dog.

1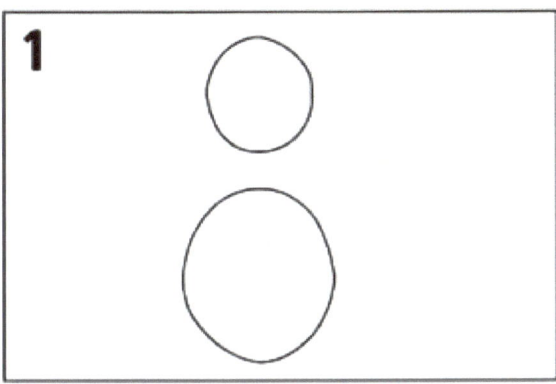

2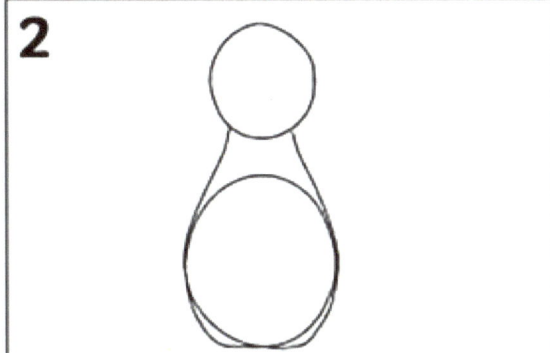

3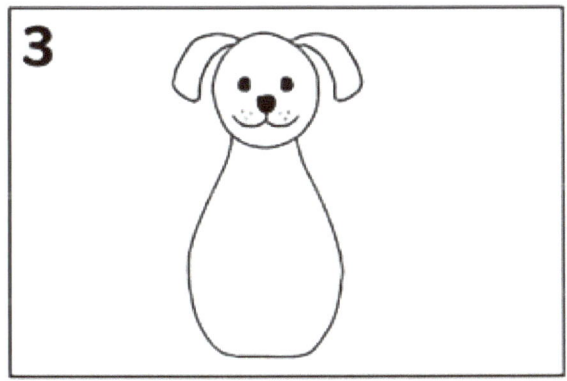

4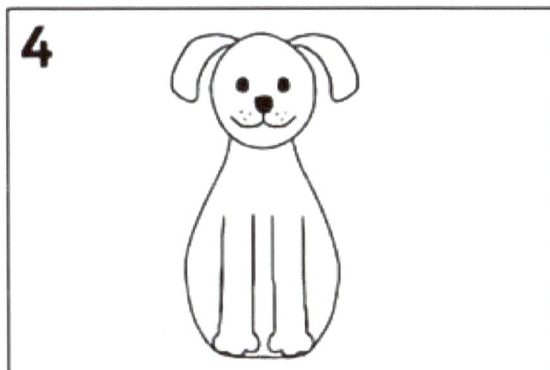

5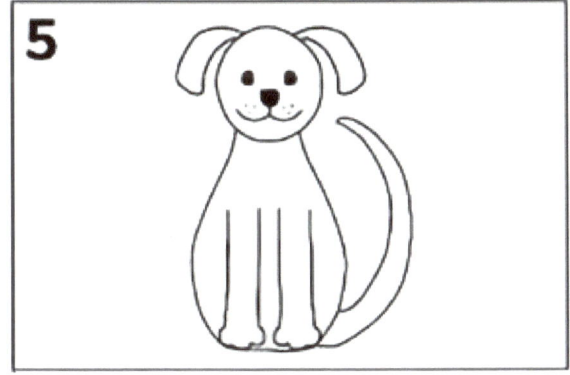

6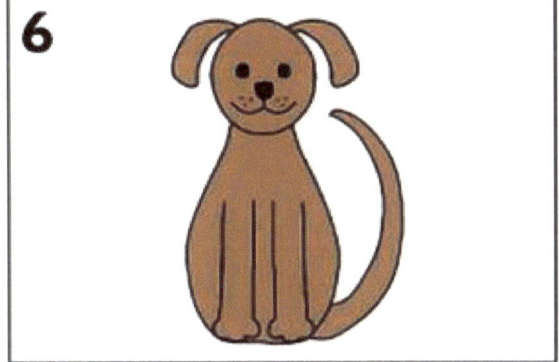

How to Draw a Sheep

Use these instructions to help you draw a simple cartoon sheep:

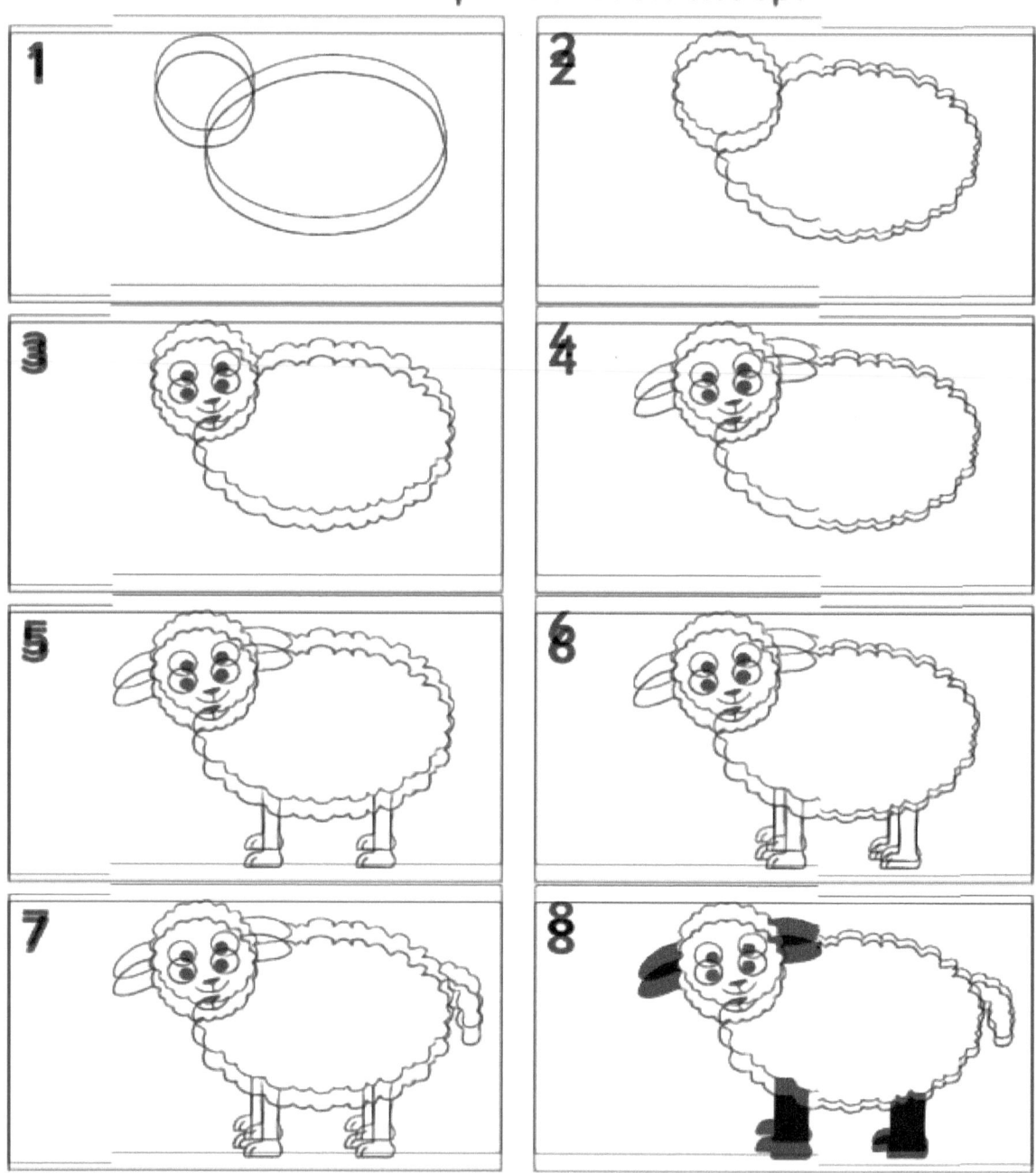

How to Draw a Cow

Use these instructions to help you draw a simple cartoon cow:

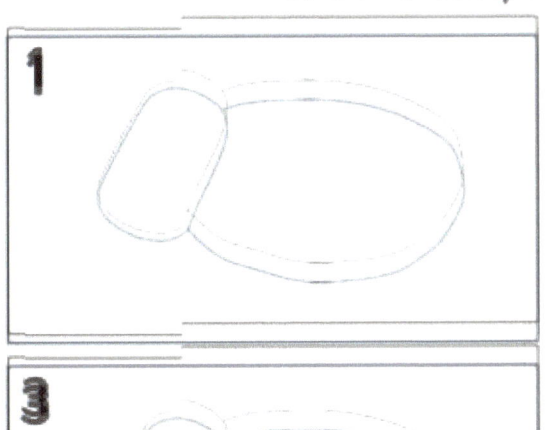
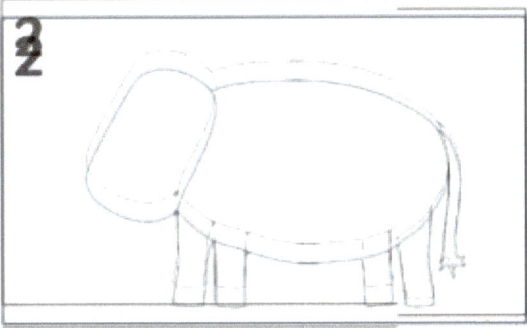
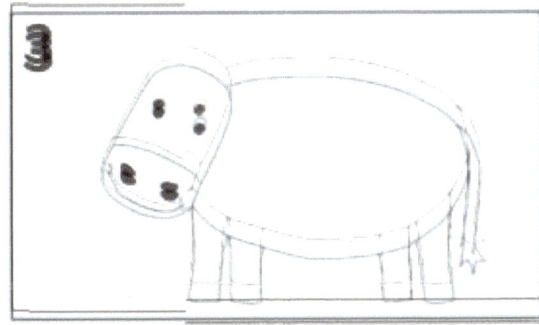
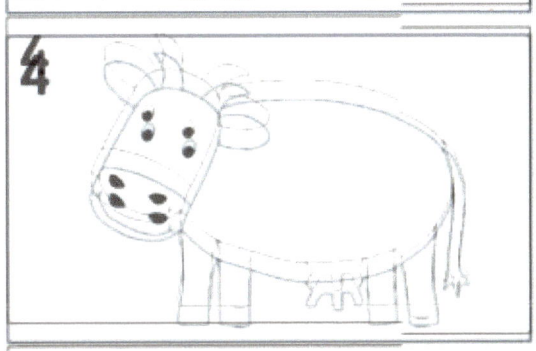
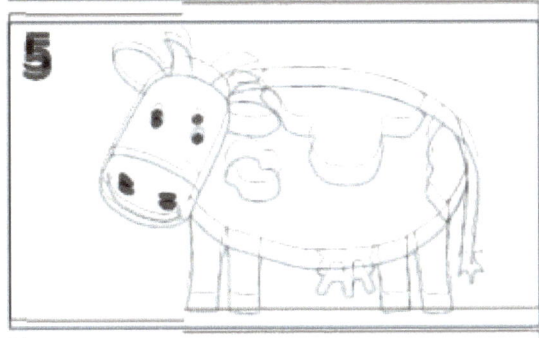
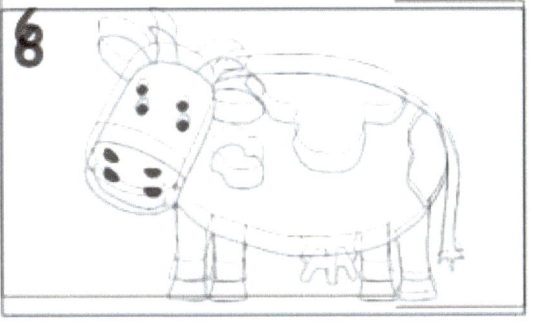
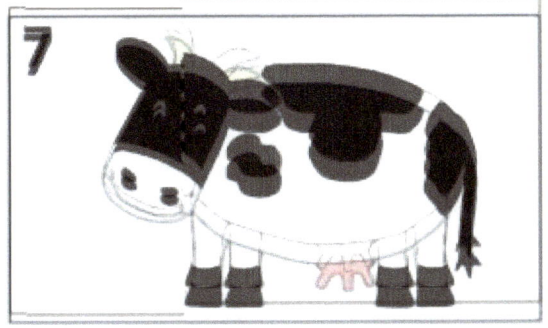

How to Draw an Elephant

Use these instructions to help you draw a simple cartoon elephant.

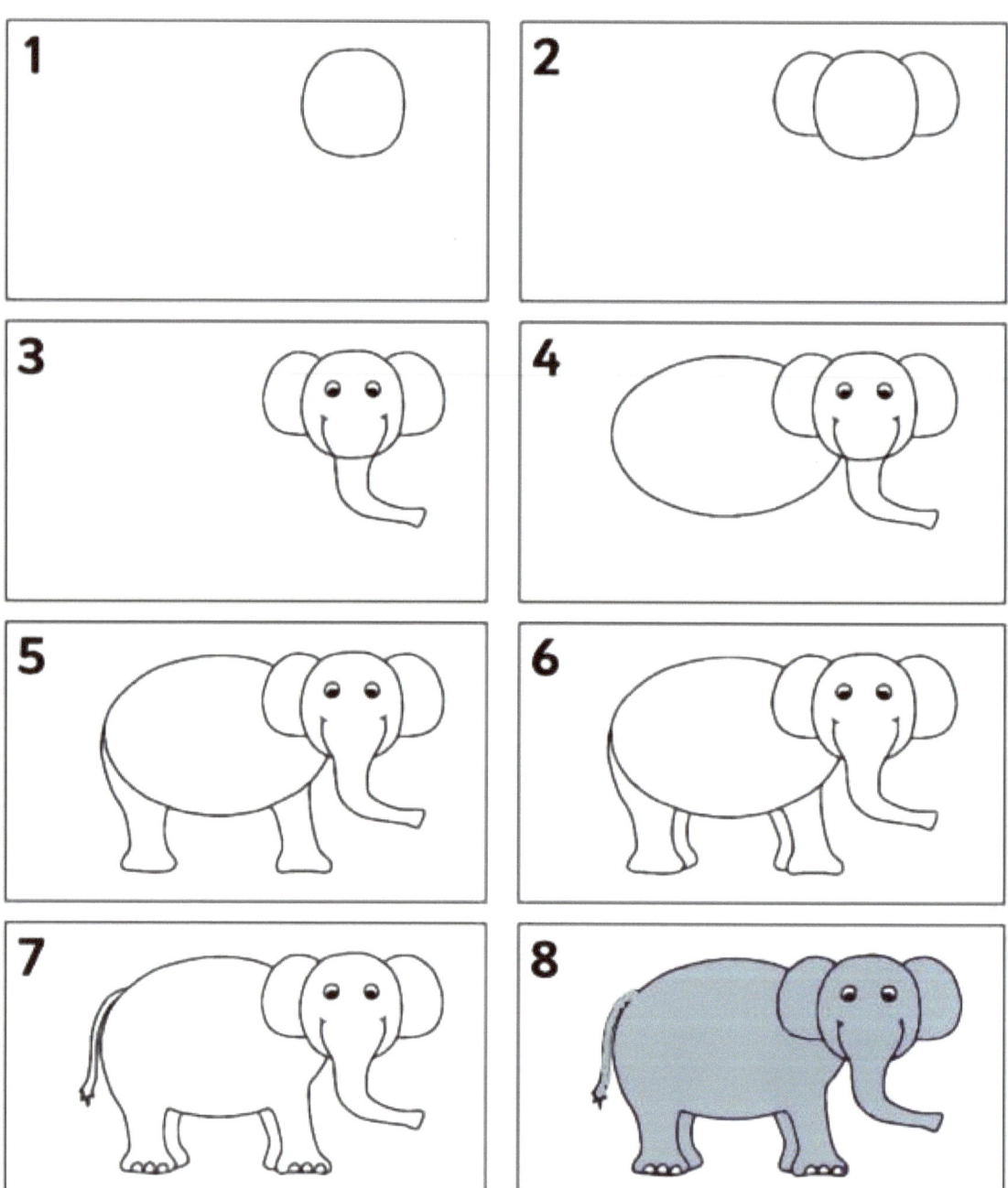

How to Draw a Penguin

Use these instructions to help you draw a simple cartoon penguin.

1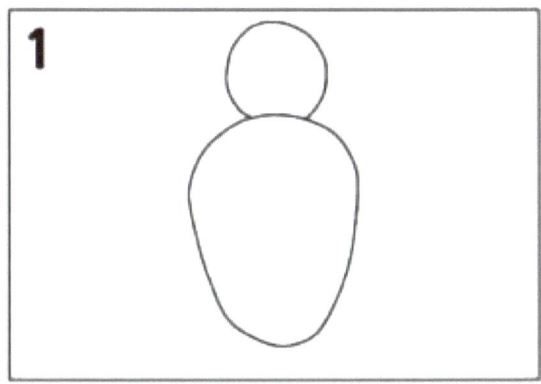

2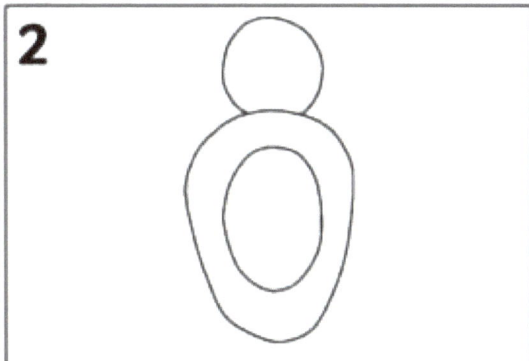

3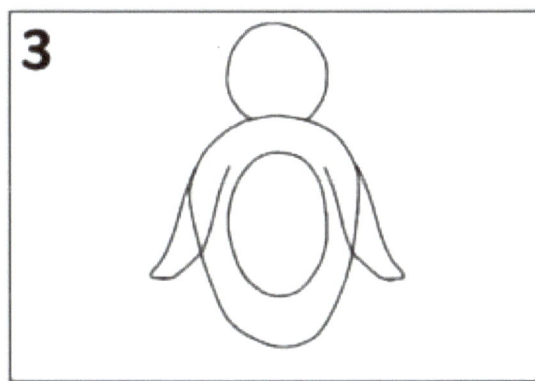

4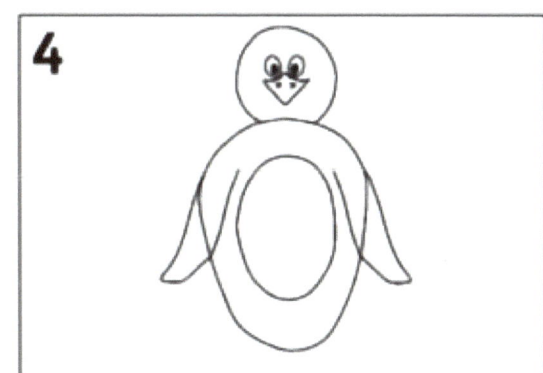

5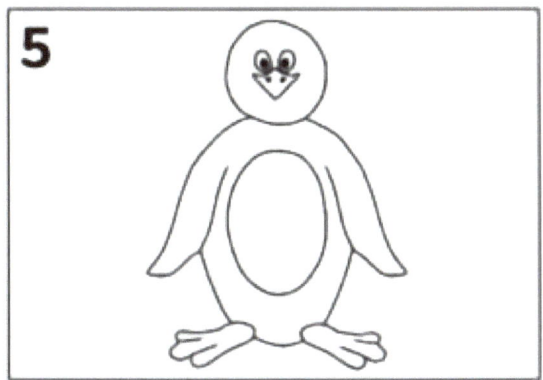

6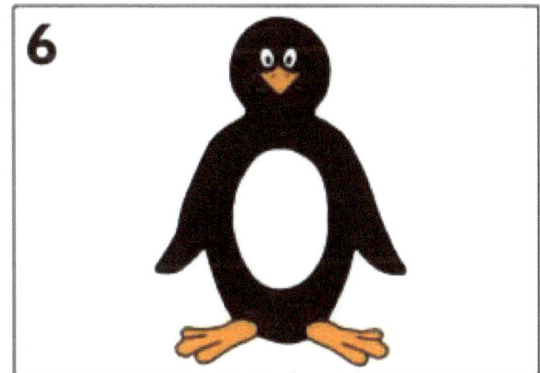

How to Draw a Dinosaur

Use these instructions to help you draw a simple cartoon stegosaurus.

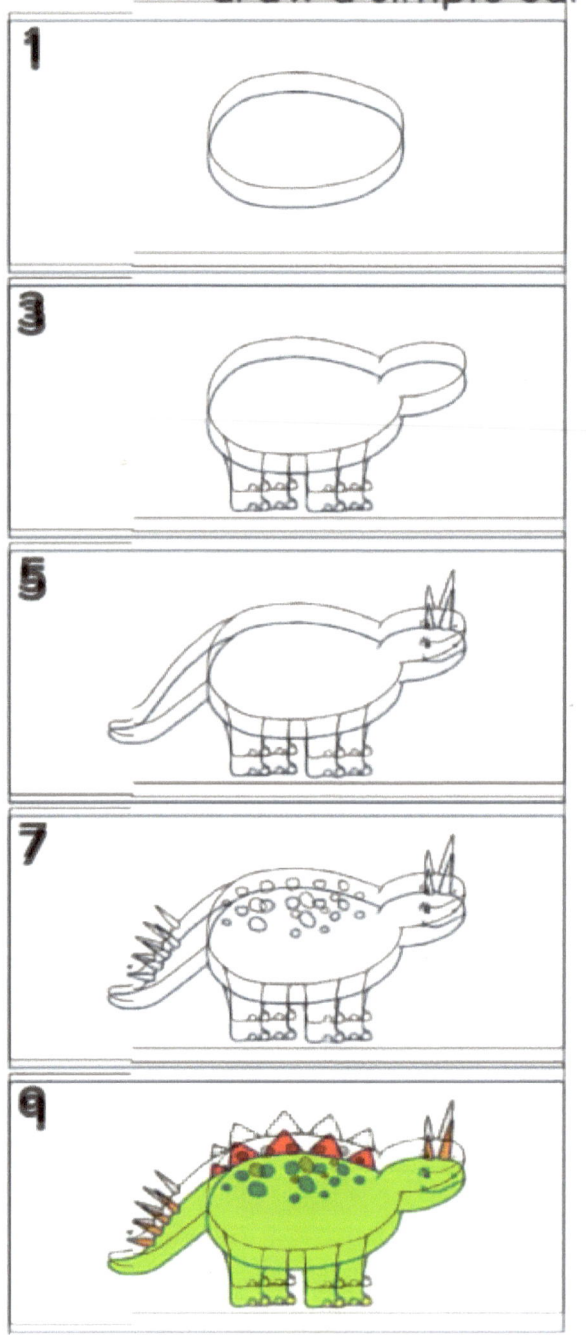
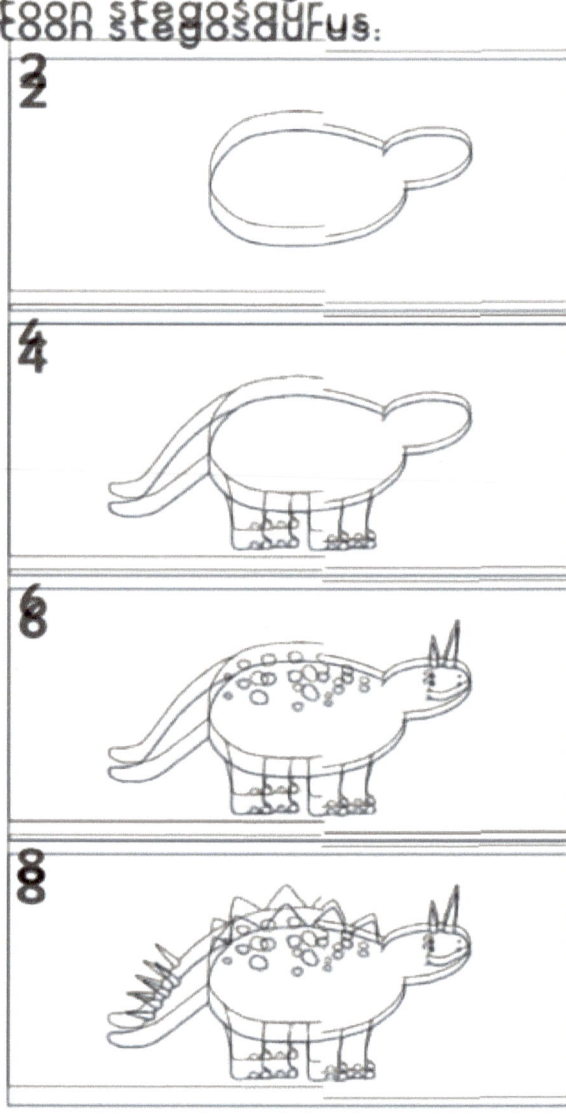

How to Draw a Butterfly

Use these instructions to help you draw a simple butterfly:

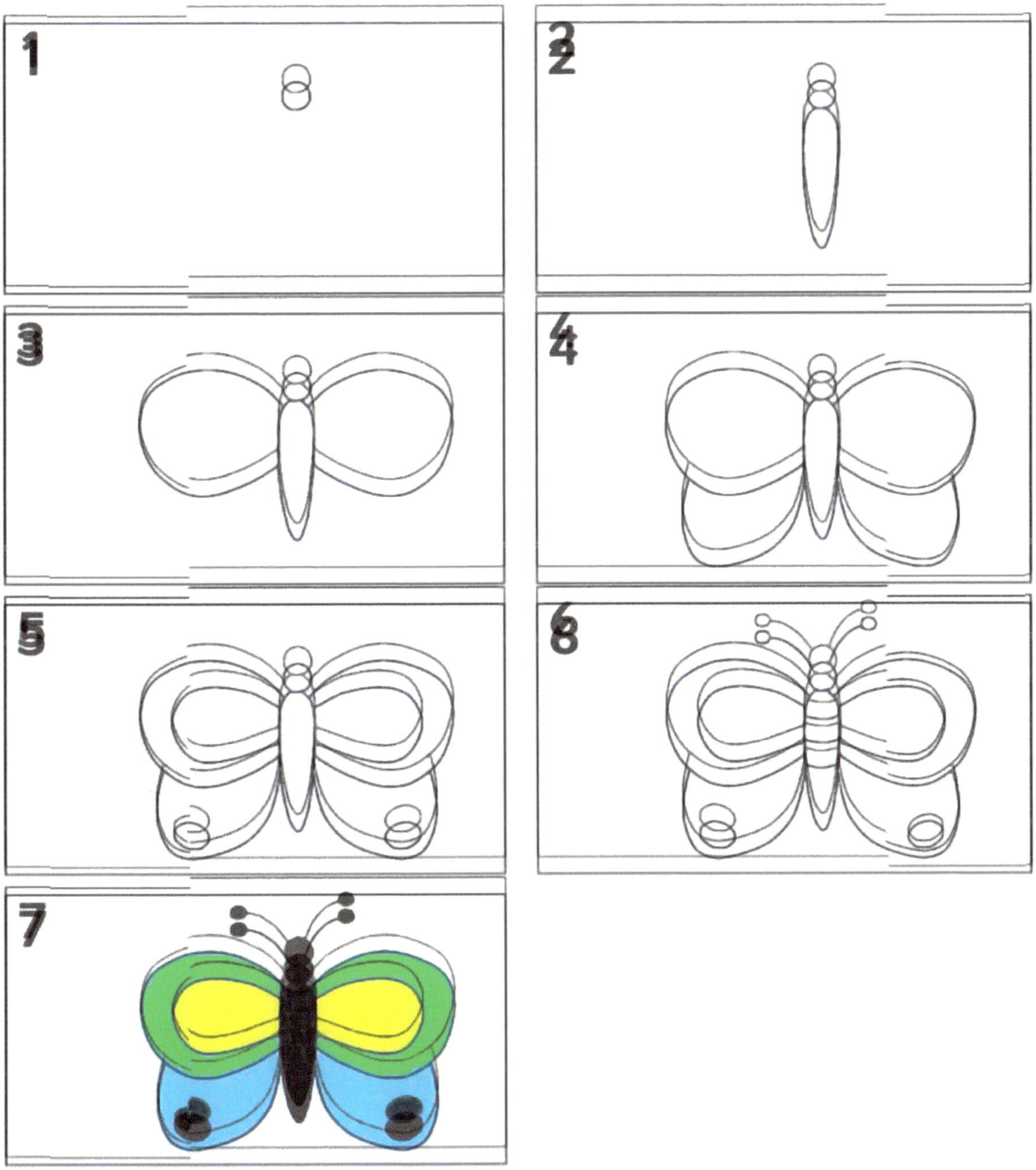

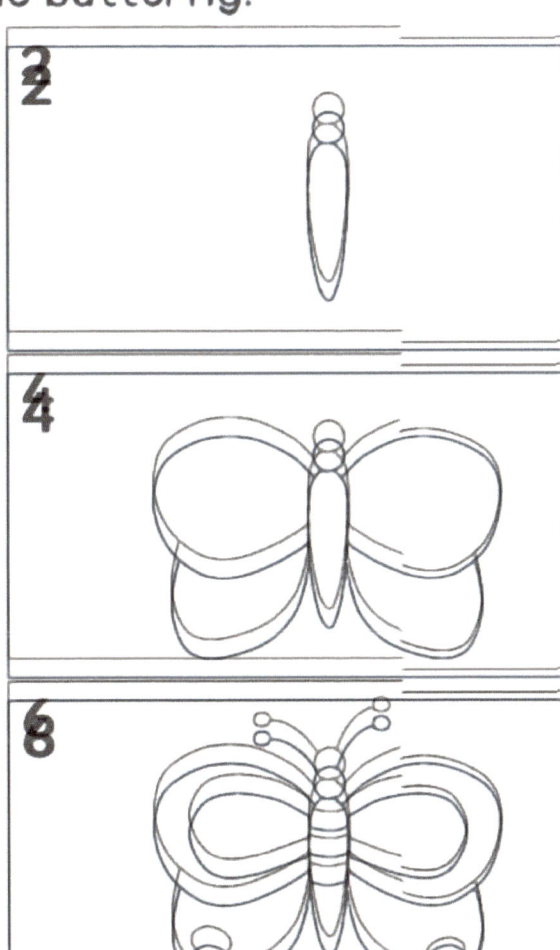

How to Draw a Bear

Use these instructions to help you draw a simple bear.

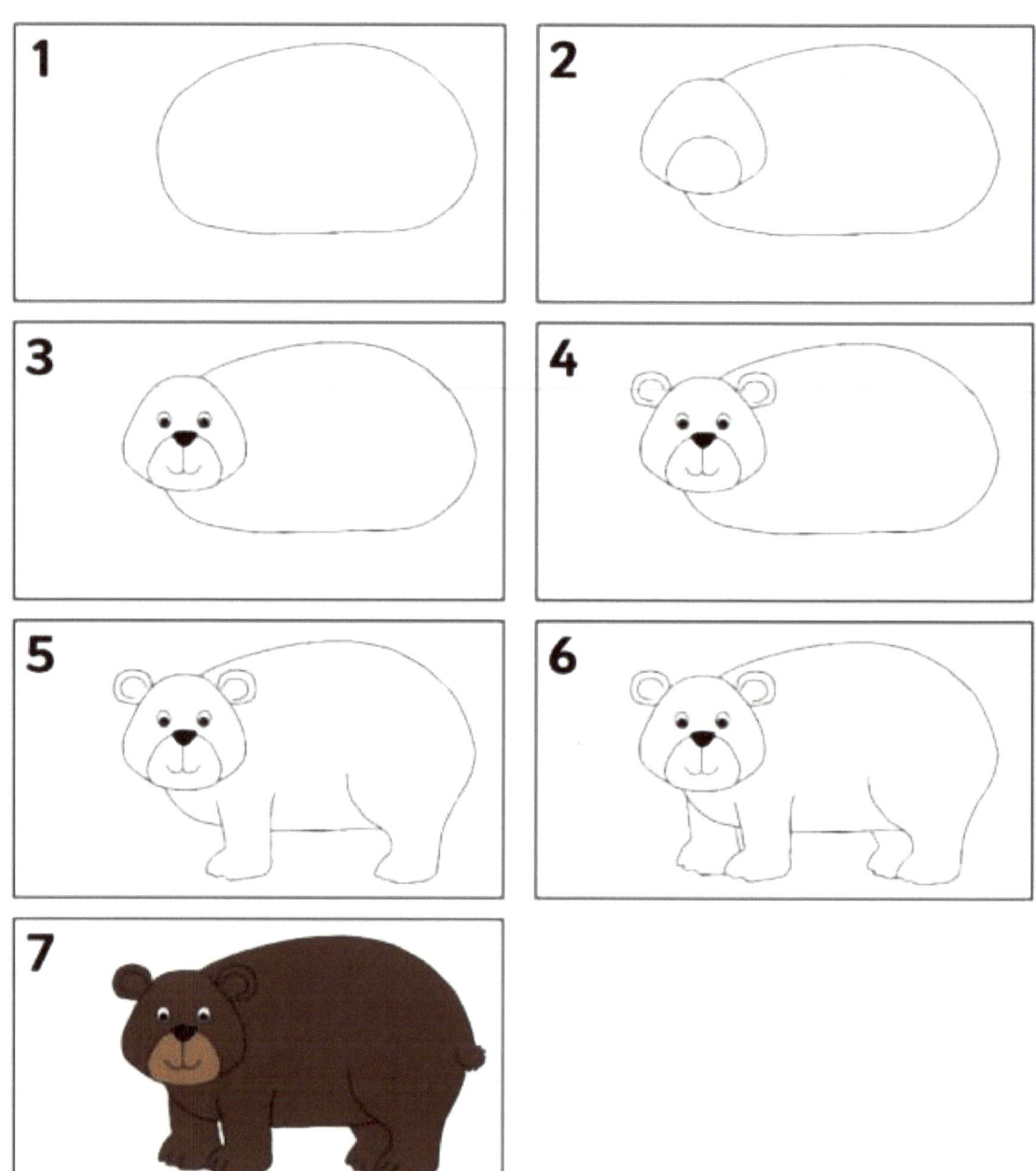

How to Draw an Owl

Use these instructions to help you draw a simple cartoon owl.

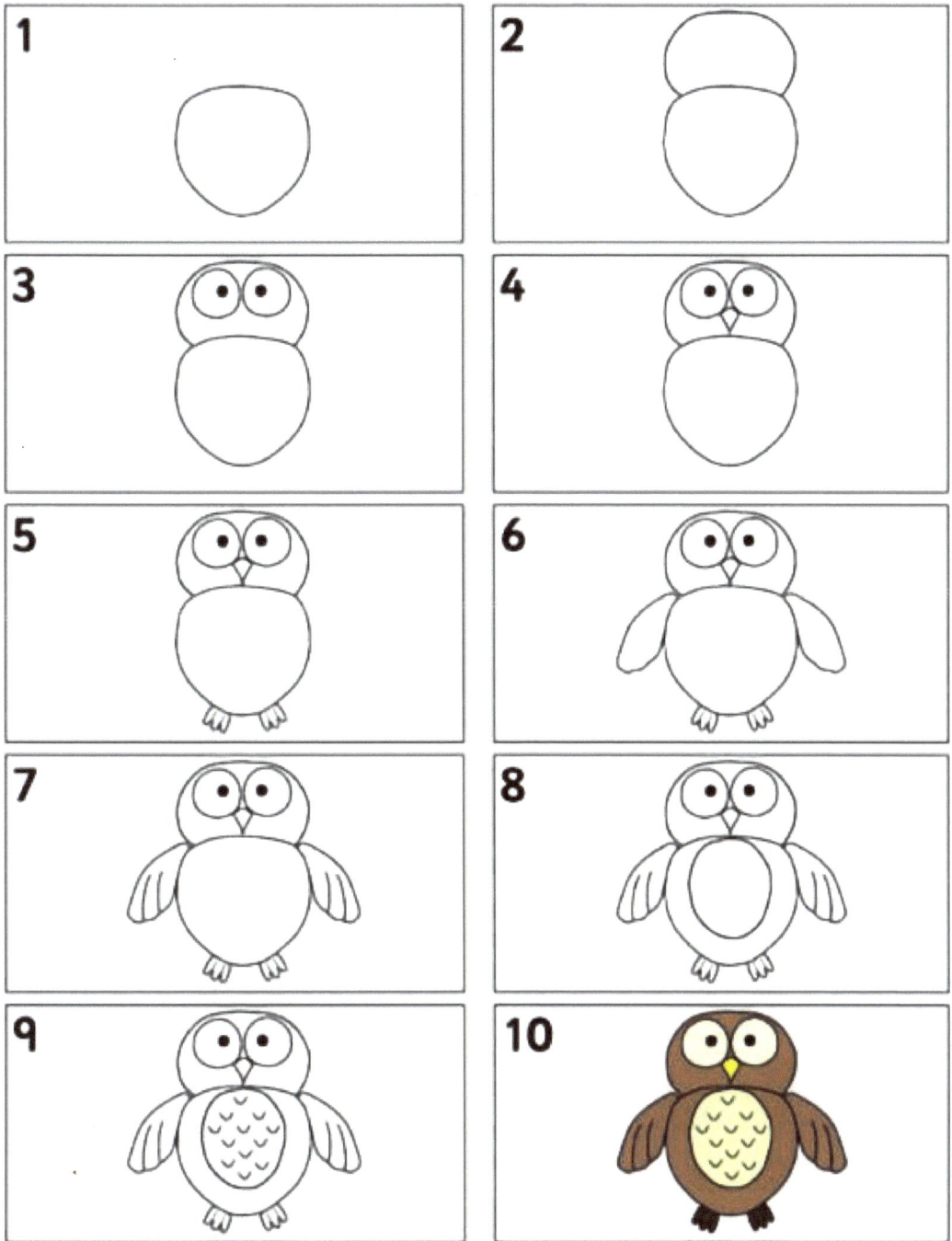

How to Draw a Crab

Use these instructions to help you draw a simple cartoon crab:

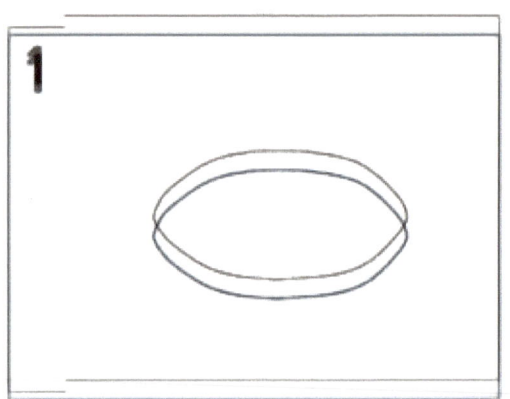
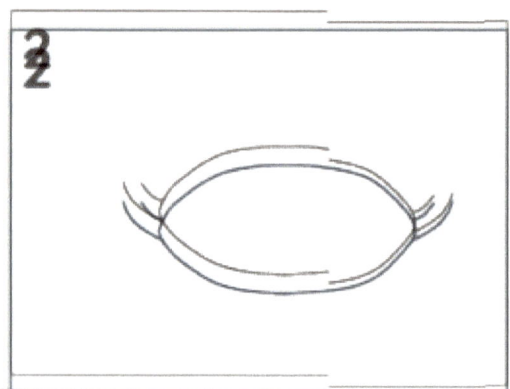
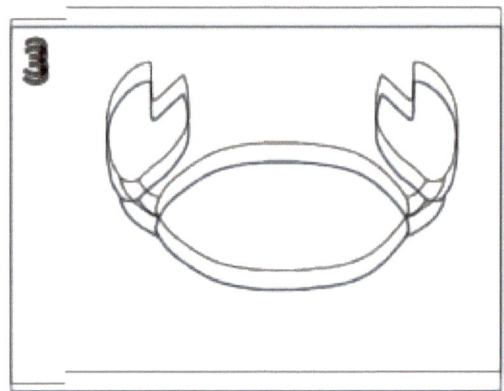
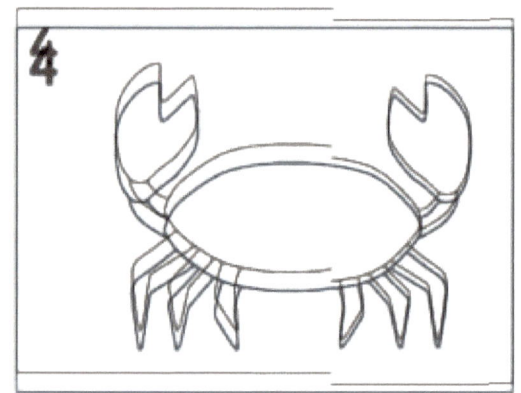
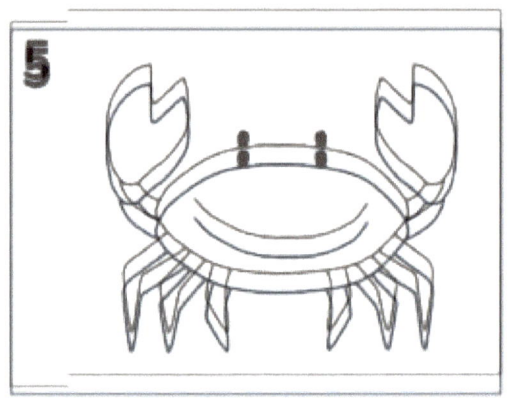
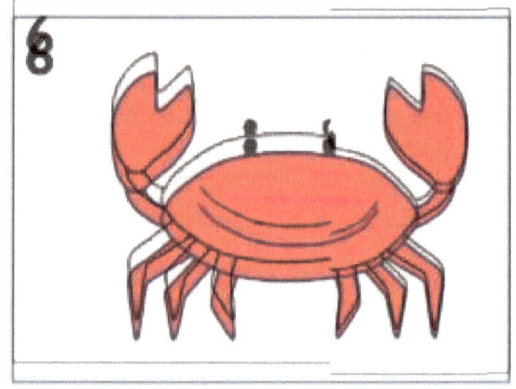

How to Draw a Bird
Use these instructions to help you draw a simple bird:

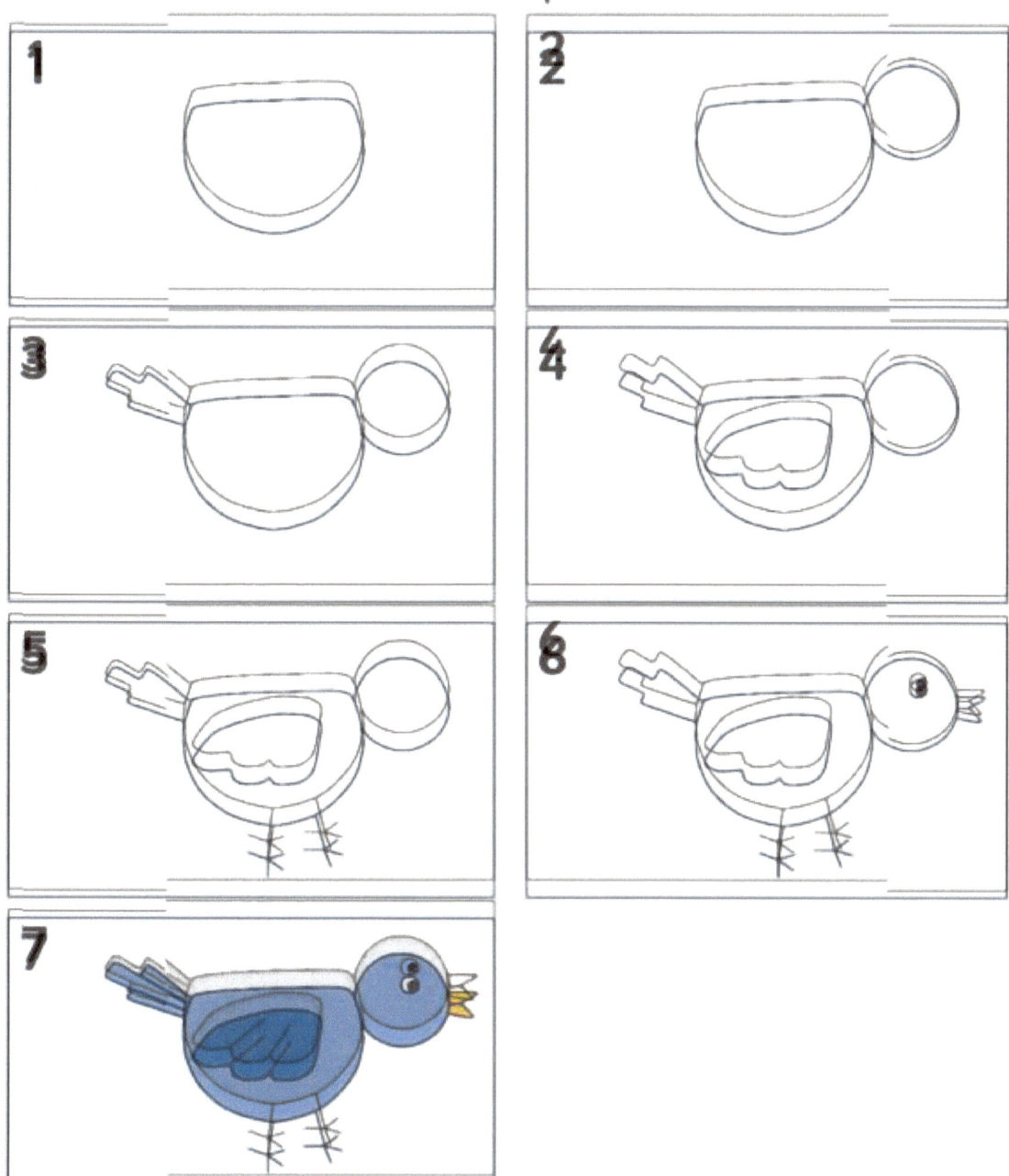

How to Draw a Polar Bear

Use these instructions to help you draw a simple cartoon polar bear.

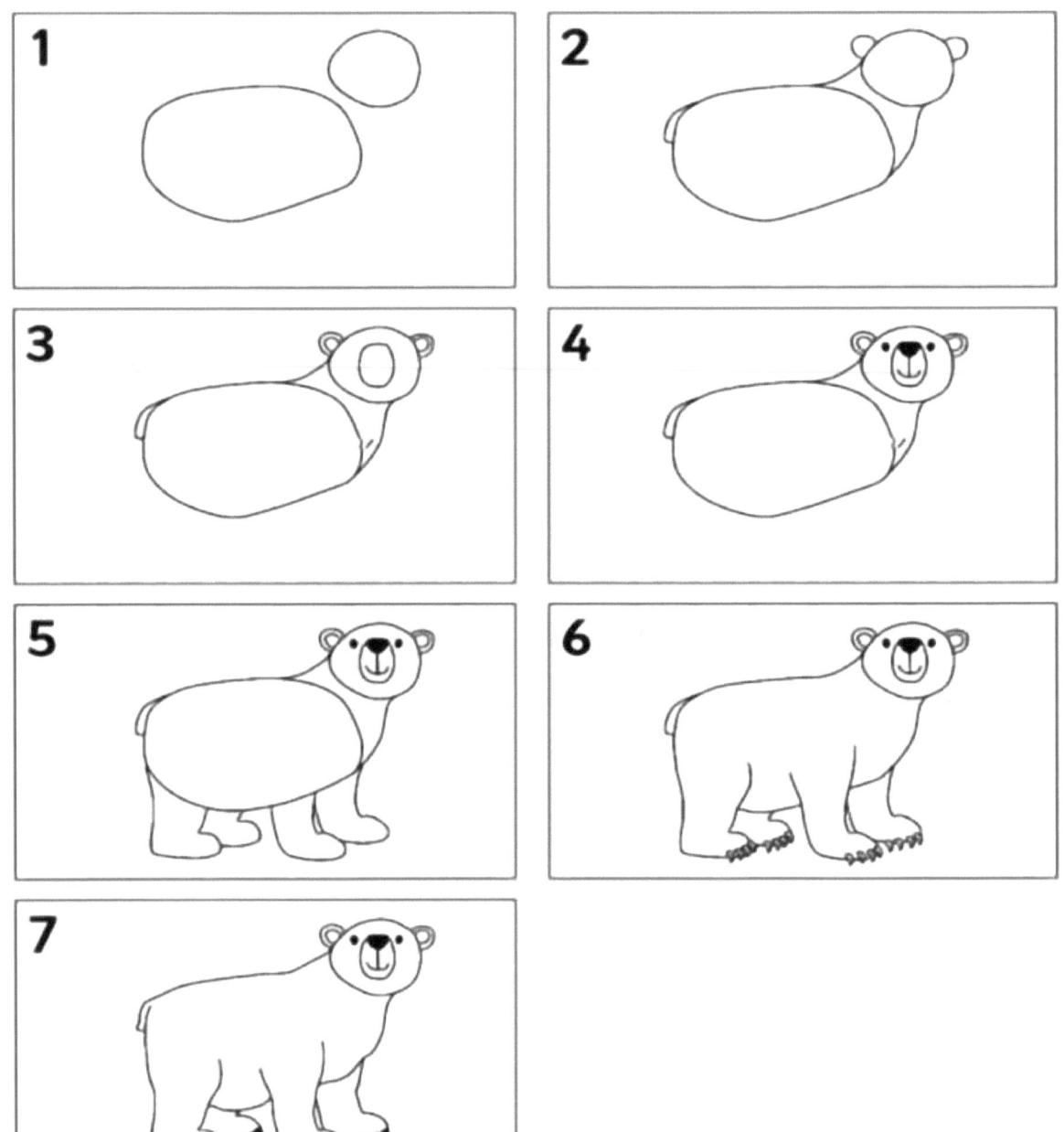

How to Draw a Bee

Use these instructions to help you draw a simple cartoon bee.

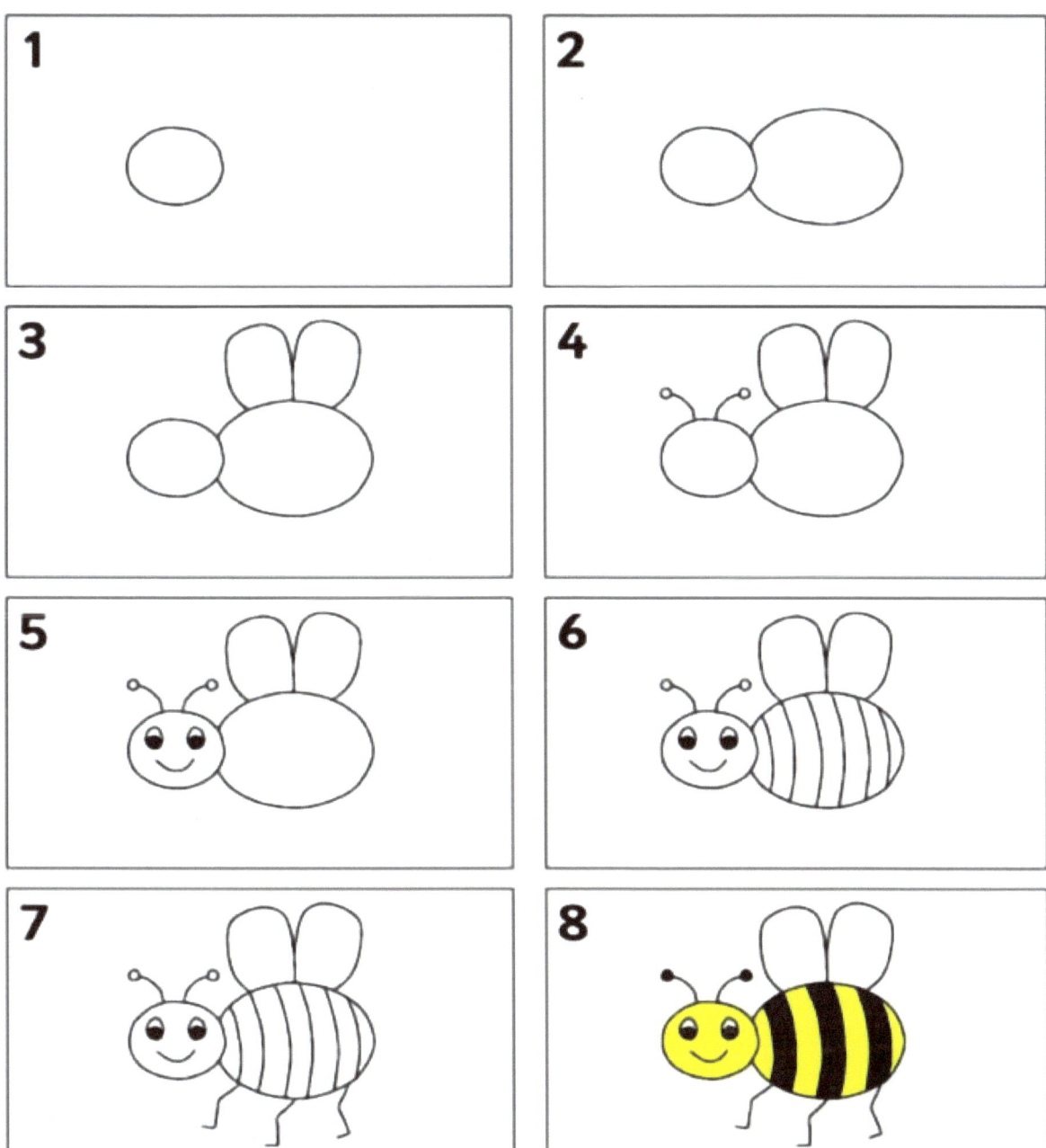

How to Draw a Chick

Use these instructions to help you draw a simple cartoon chick:

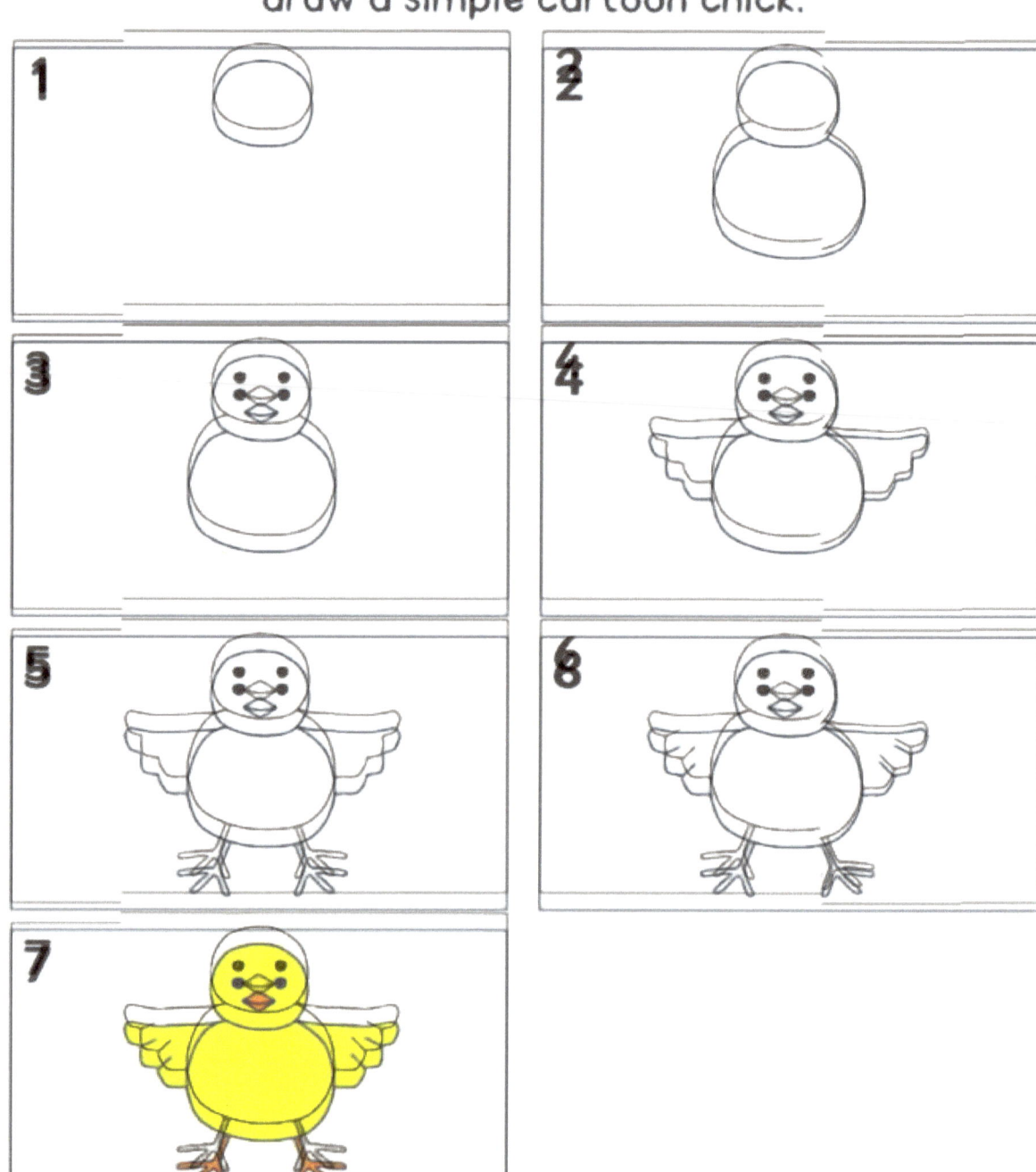

How to Draw a Caterpillar

Use these instructions to help you draw a simple caterpillar:

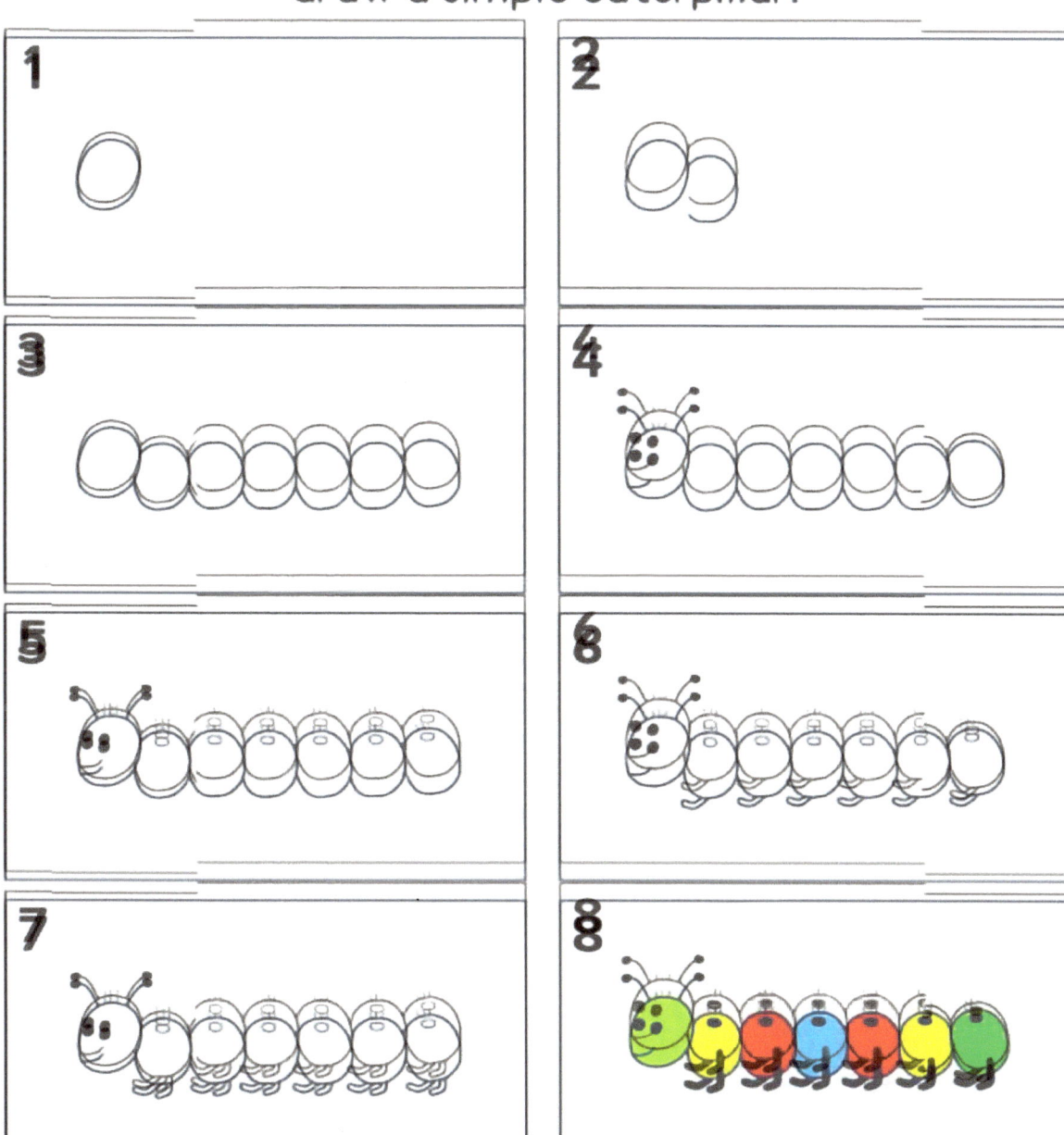

How to Draw a Giraffe

Use these instructions to help you draw a simple cartoon giraffe.

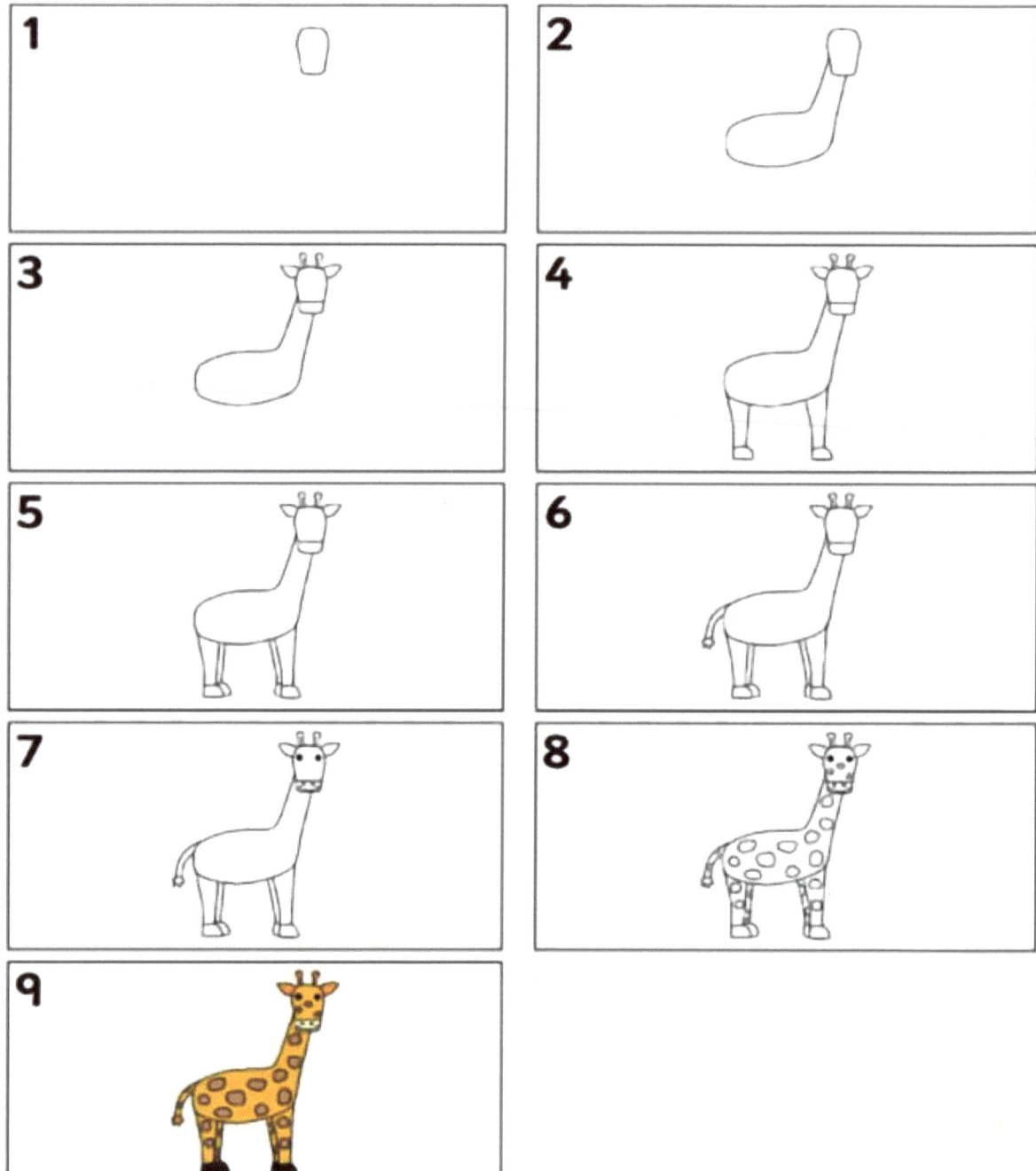

How to Draw a Peacock

Use these instructions to help you draw a simple peacock.

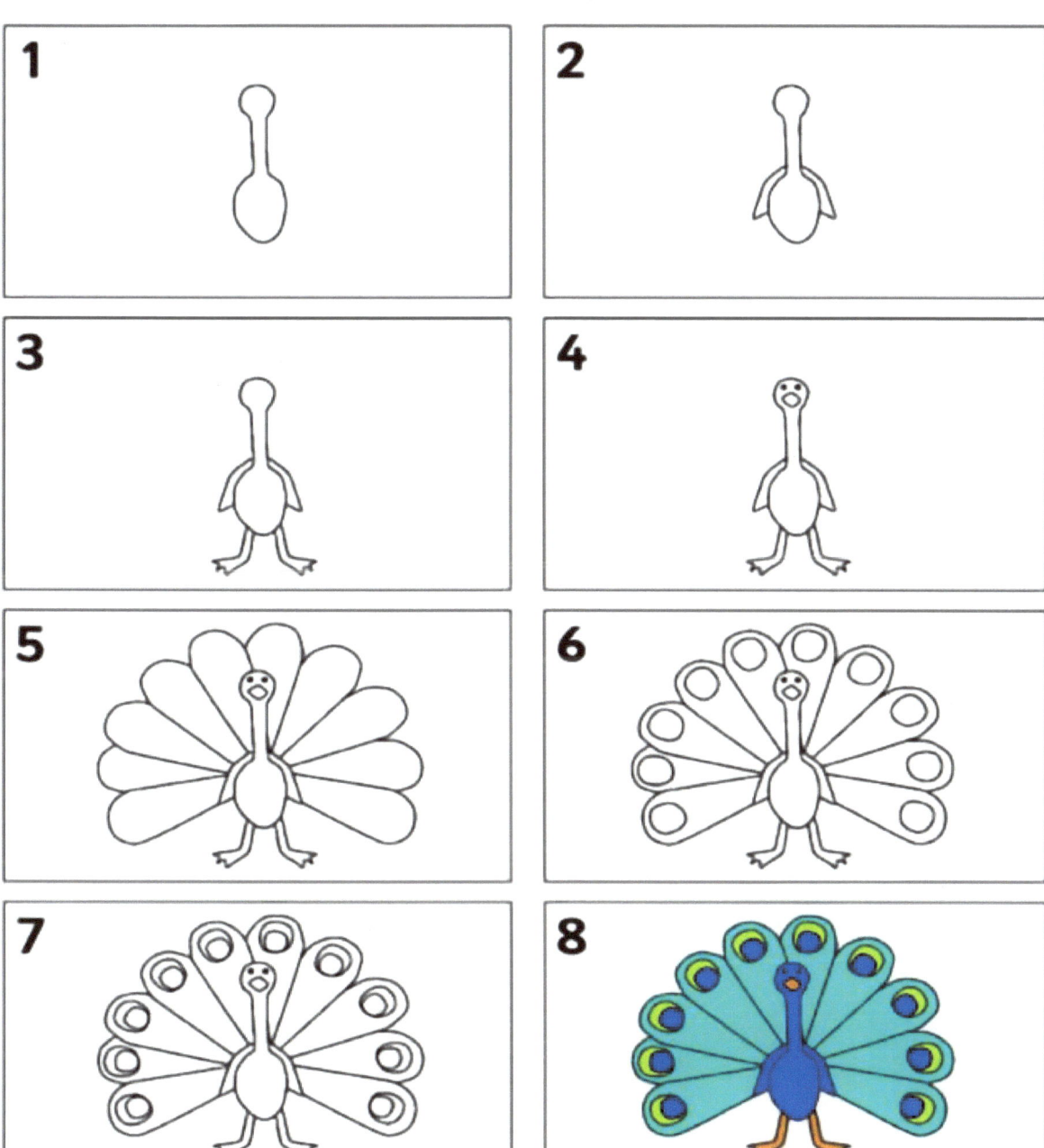

How to Draw a Monkey

Use these instructions to help you draw a simple monkey:

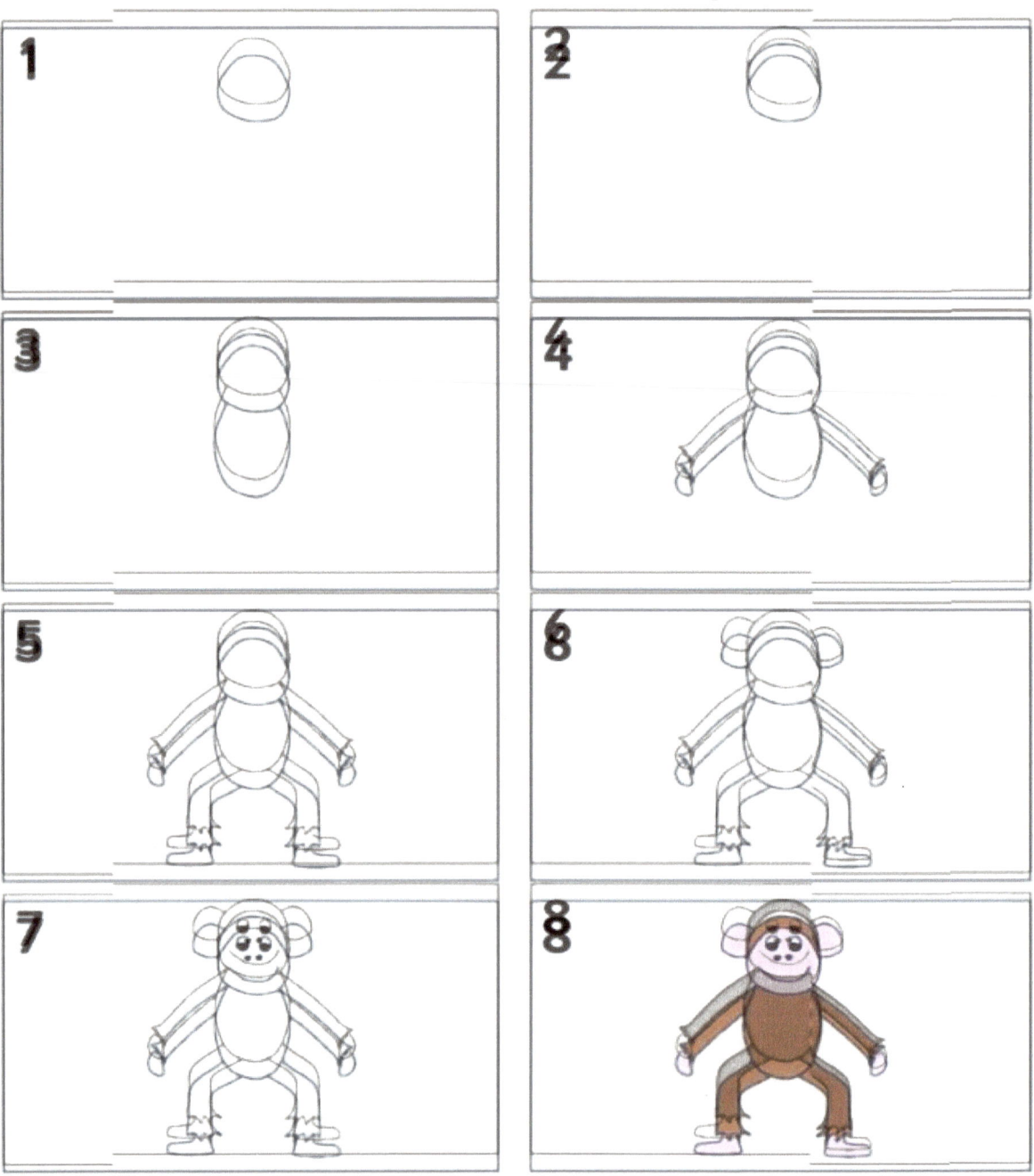

How to Draw a Camel

Use these instructions to help you draw a simple camel.

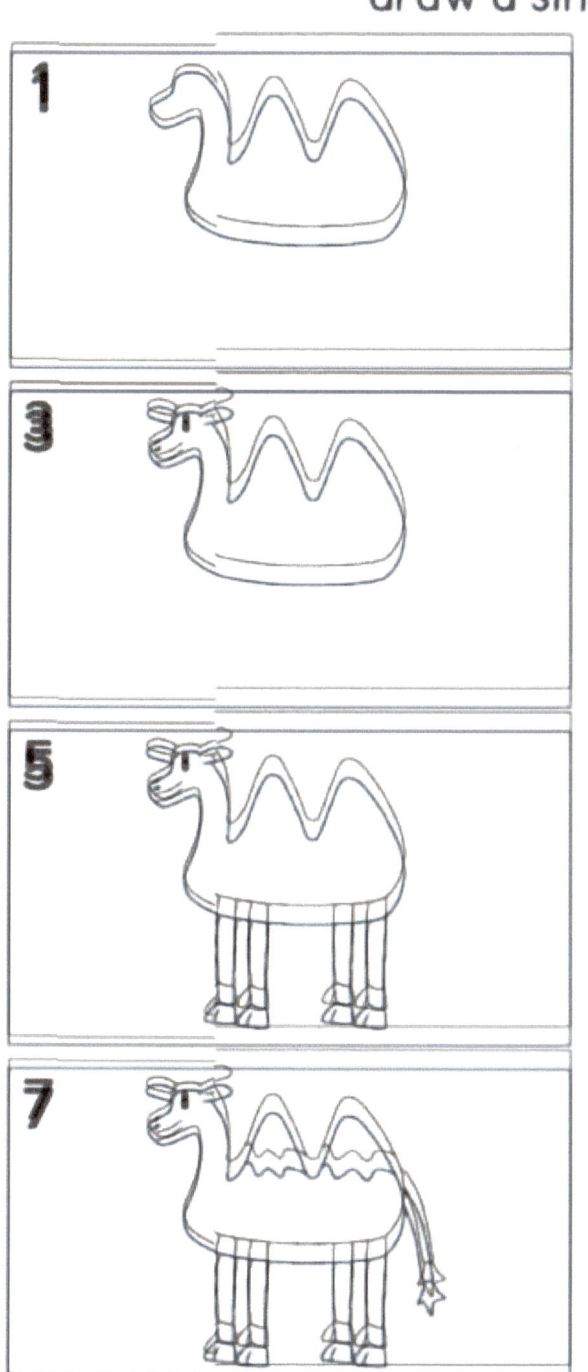
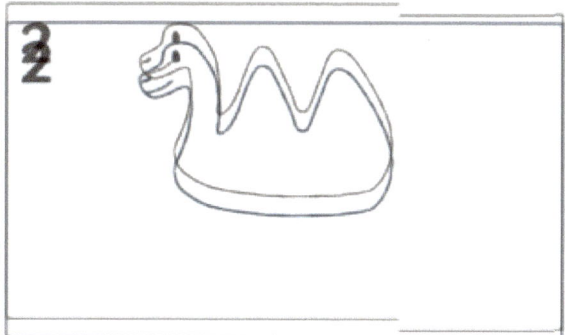
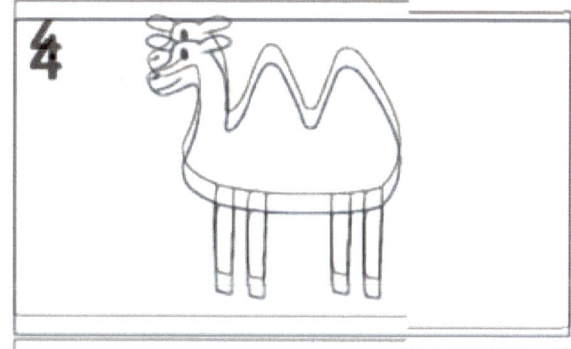
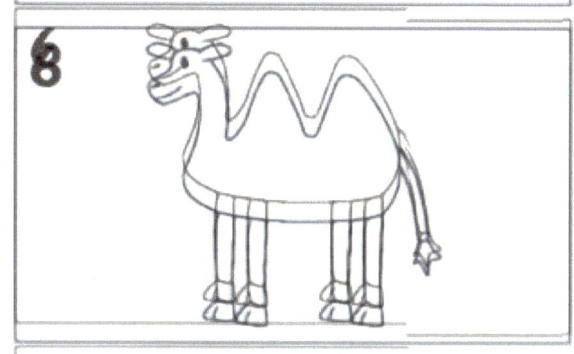
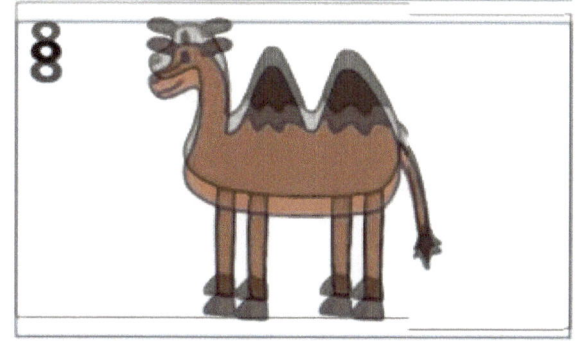

How to Draw a Hippo

Use these instructions to help you draw a simple hippopotamus.

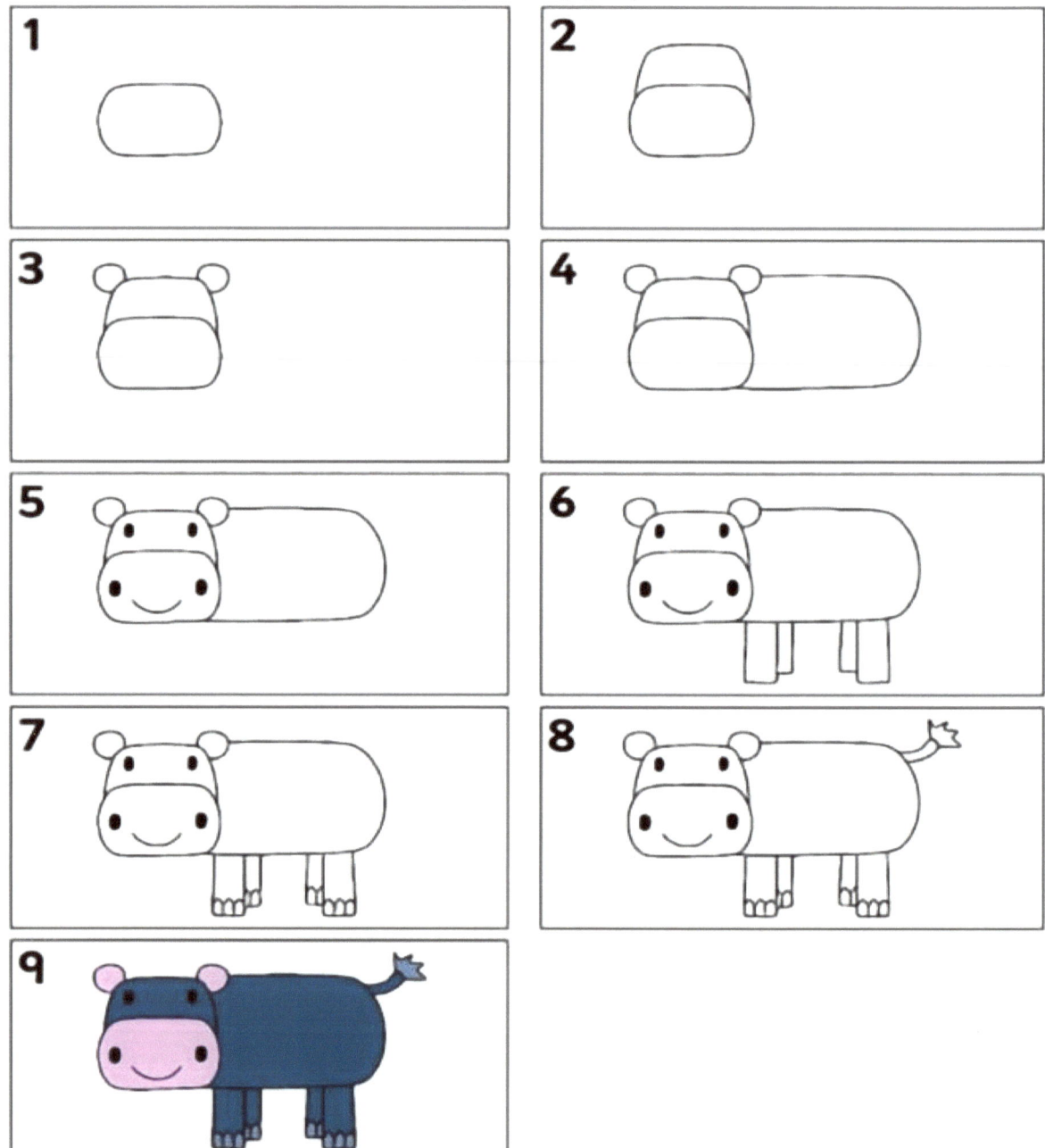

How to Draw a Ladybird

Use these instructions to help you draw a simple ladybird.

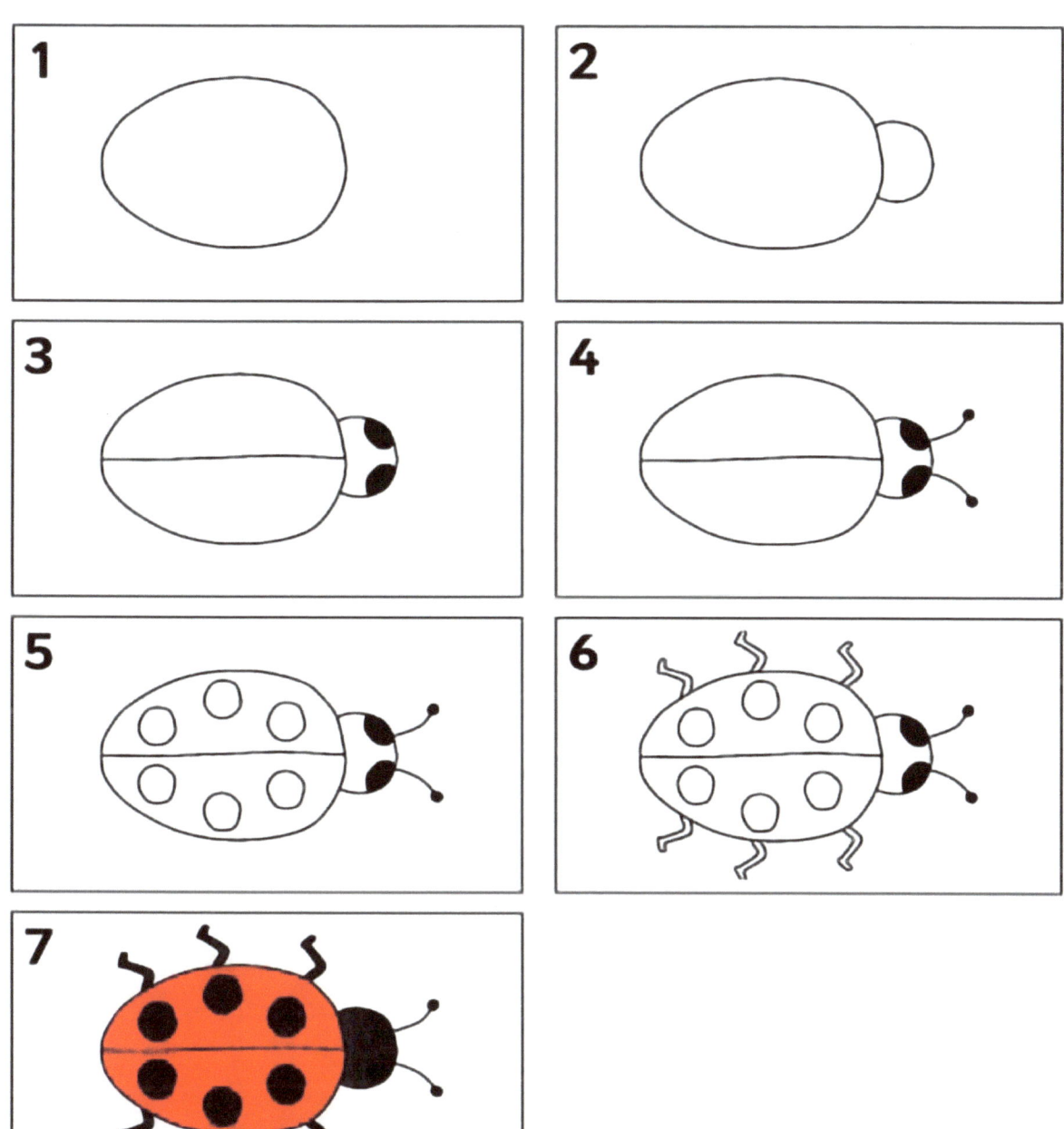

How to Draw a Jellyfish

Use these instructions to help you draw a simple cartoon jellyfish.

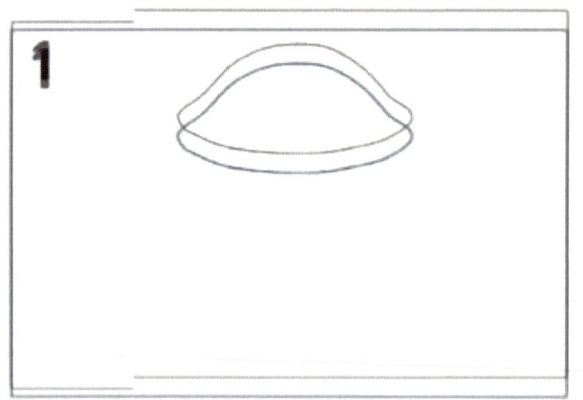
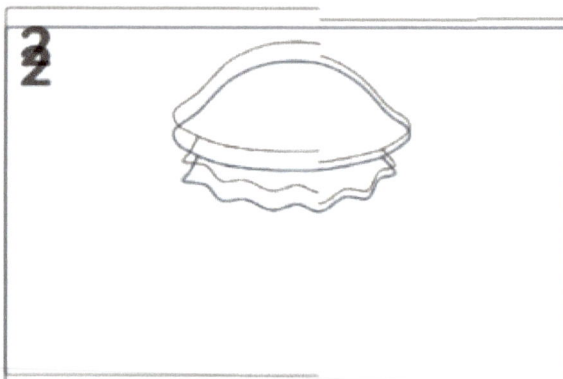
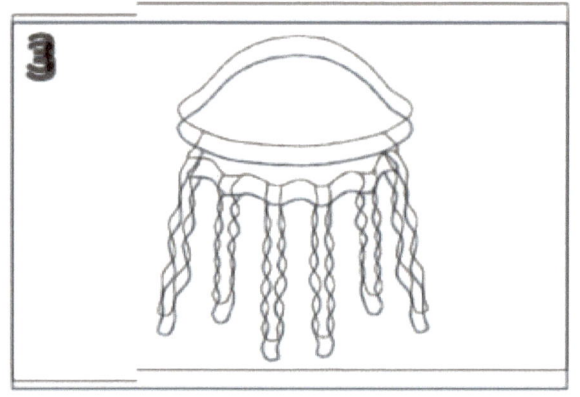
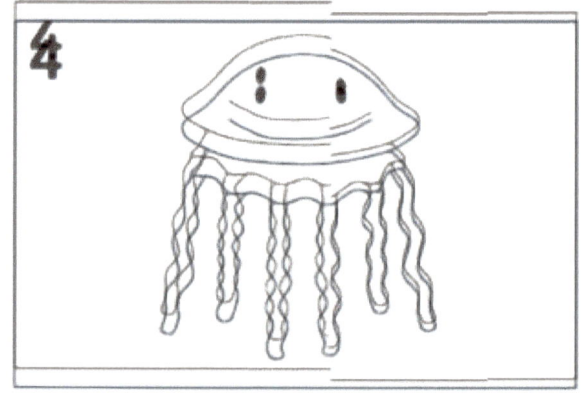
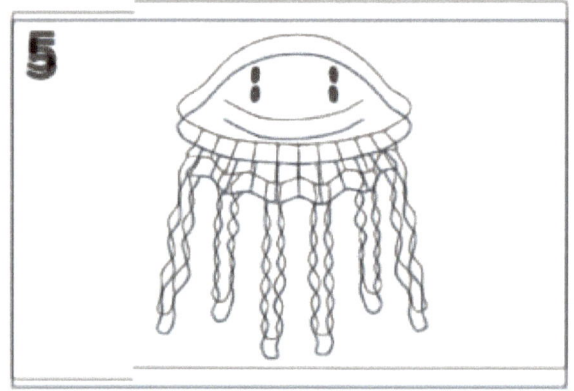
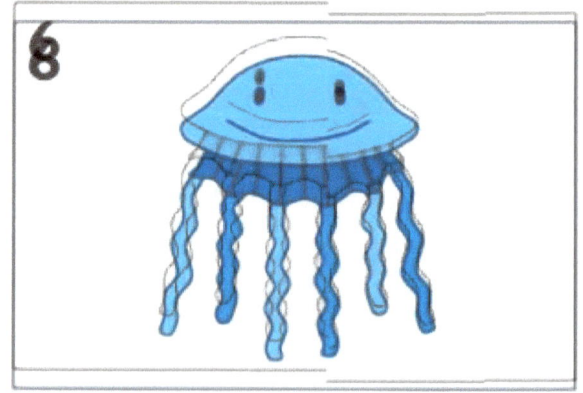

You are an artist now

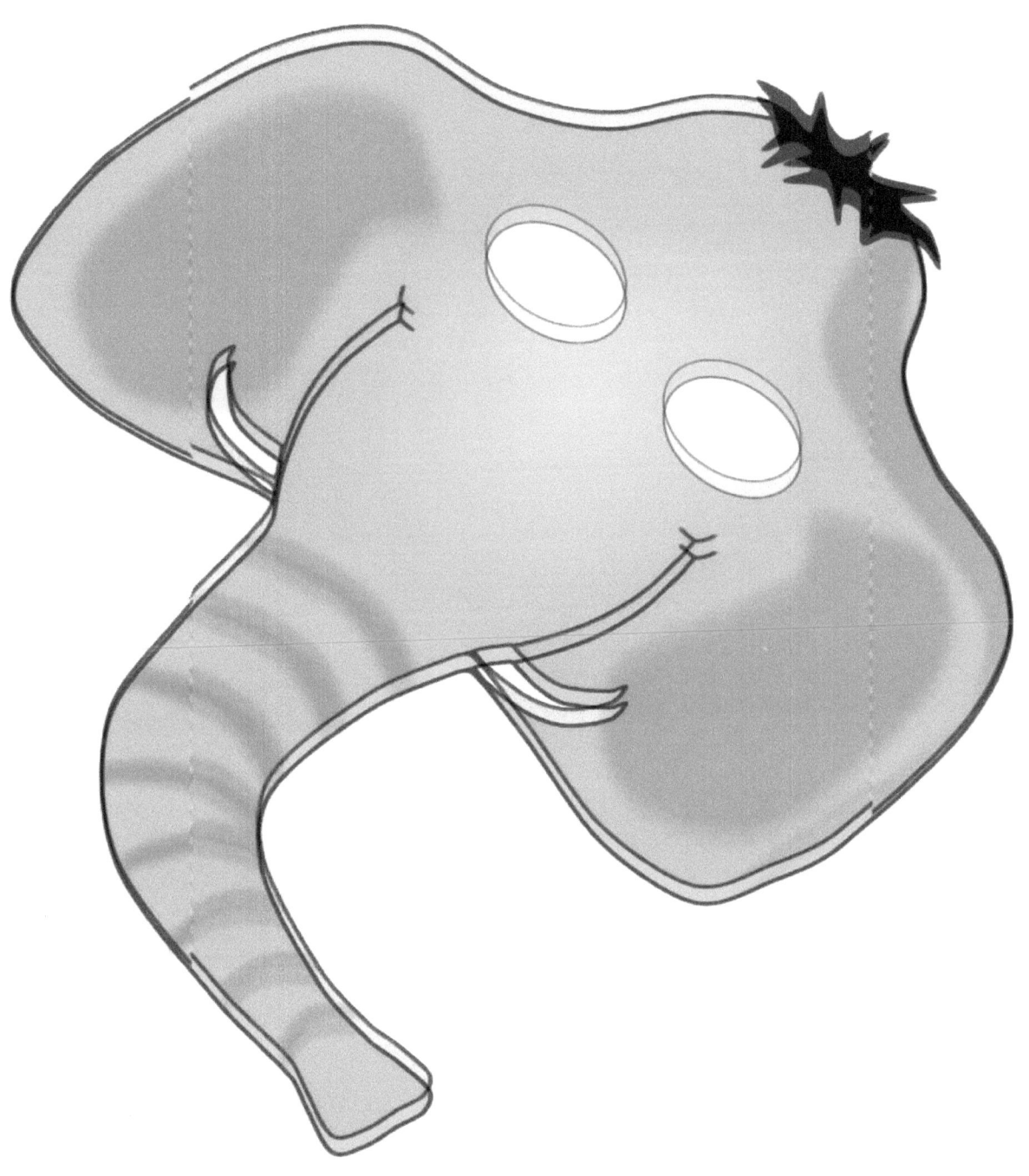

You can do it

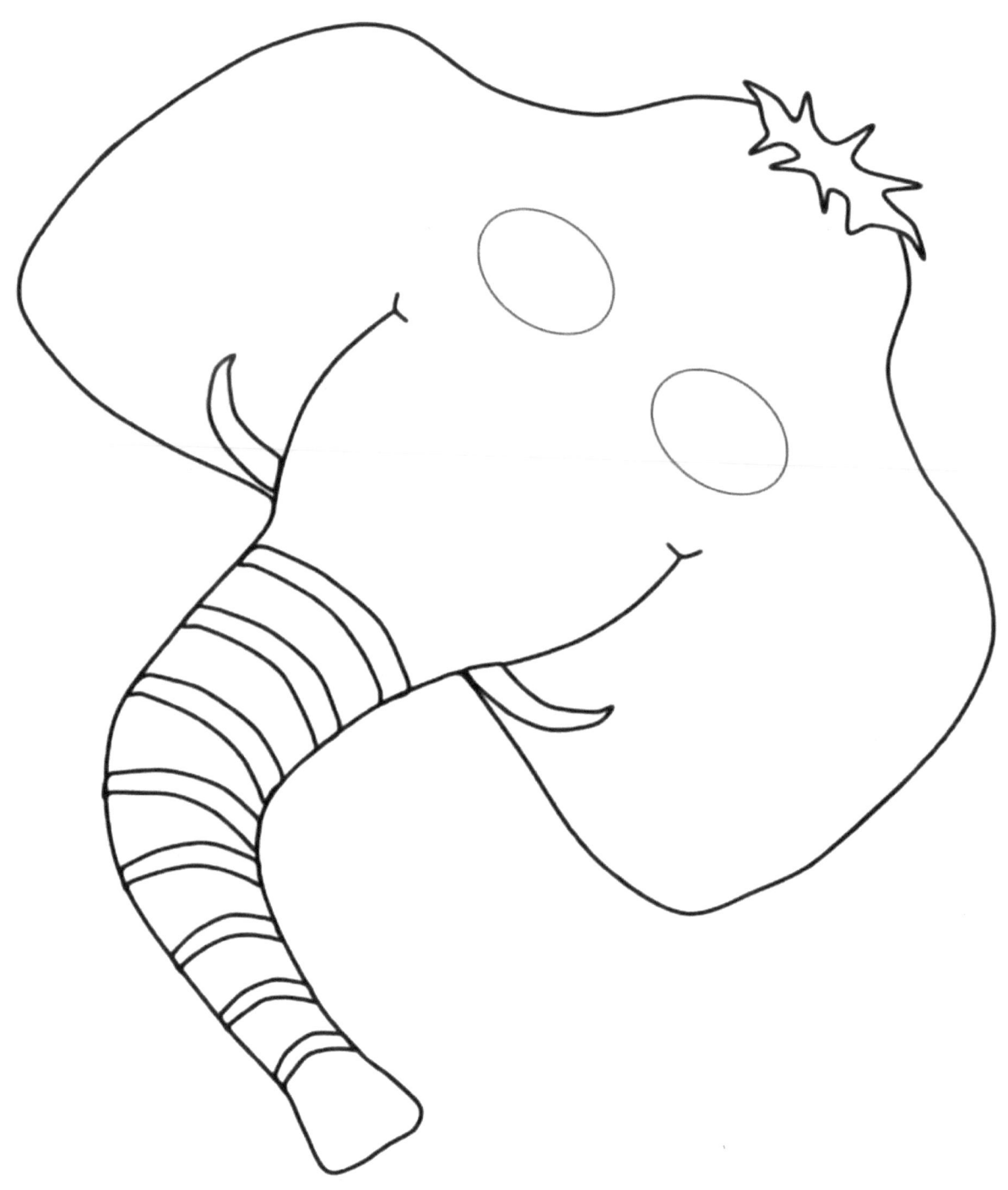

Congratulation your first month is **DONE**

www.ingramcontent.com/pod-product-compliance
Lightning Source LLC
Chambersburg PA
CBHW051939210526
45473CB00006B/2302